A SHORT HISTORY OF ENGLAND

G. K. CHESTERTON

CONTENTS

A SHORT HISTORY OF ENGLAND

1. INTRODUCTION

It will be very reasonably asked why I should consent, though upon a sort of challenge, to write even a popular essay in English history, who make no pretence to particular scholarship and am merely a member of the public. The answer is that I know just enough to know one thing: that a history from the standpoint of a member of the public has not been written. What we call the popular histories should rather be called the anti-popular histories. They are all, nearly without exception, written against the people; and in them the populace is either ignored or elaborately proved to have been wrong. It is true that Green called his book "A Short History of the English People"; but he seems to have thought it too short for the people to be properly mentioned. For instance, he calls one very large part of his story "Puritan England." But England never was Puritan. It would have been almost as unfair to call the rise of Henry of Navarre "Puritan France." And some of our extreme Whig historians would have been pretty nearly capable of calling the campaign of Wexford and Drogheda "Puritan Ireland."

But it is especially in the matter of the Middle Ages that the popular histories trample upon the popular traditions. In this respect there is an almost comic contrast between the general information provided about England in the last two or three centuries, in which its present industrial system was being built up, and the general information given about the preceding centuries, which we call broadly mediæval. Of the sort of waxwork history which is thought sufficient for the side-show of the age of abbots and crusaders, a small instance will be sufficient. A popular Encyclopædia appeared some years ago, professing among other things to teach English History to the masses; and in this I came upon a series of pictures of the English kings. No one could expect them to be all authentic; but the interest attached to those that were necessarily imaginary. There is much vivid material in contemporary literature for portraits of men like Henry II. or Edward I.; but this did not seem to have been found, or even sought. And wandering to the image that stood for Stephen of Blois, my eye was staggered by a gentleman with one of those helmets with steel brims curved like a crescent, which went with the age of ruffs and trunk-hose. I am tempted to suspect that the head was that of a halberdier at some such scene as the execution of Mary Queen of Scots. But he had a helmet; and helmets were mediæval; and any old helmet was good enough for Stephen.

Now suppose the readers of that work of reference had looked for the portrait of Charles I. and found the head of a policeman. Suppose it had been taken, modern helmet and all, out of some snapshot in the *Daily Sketch* of the arrest of Mrs. Pankhurst. I think we may go so far as to say that the readers would have refused to accept it as a lifelike portrait of Charles I. They would have formed the opinion that there must be some mistake. Yet the time that elapsed between Stephen and Mary was much longer than the time that has elapsed between Charles and ourselves. The revolution in human society between the first of the Crusades and the last of the Tudors was immeasurably more colossal and complete than any change between Charles and ourselves. And, above all, that revolution should be the first thing and the final thing in anything calling itself a popular history. For it is the story of how our populace gained great things, but to-day has lost everything.

Now I will modestly maintain that I know more about English history than this; and that I have as much right to make a popular summary of it as the gentleman who made the crusader and the halberdier change hats. But the curious and arresting thing about the neglect, one might say the omission, of mediæval civilization in such histories as this, lies in the fact I have already noted. It is exactly the popular story that is left out of the popular history. For instance, even a working man, a carpenter or cooper or bricklayer, has been taught about the Great Charter, as something like the Great Auk, save that its almost monstrous solitude came from being before its time instead of after. He was not taught that the whole stuff of the Middle Ages was stiff with the parchment of charters; that society was once a system of charters, and of a kind much more interesting to him. The carpenter heard of one charter given to barons, and chiefly in the interest of barons; the carpenter did not hear of any of the charters given to carpenters, to coopers, to all the people like himself. Or, to take another instance, the boy and girl reading the stock simplified histories of the schools practically never heard of such a thing as a burgher, until he appears in a shirt with a noose round his neck. They certainly do not imagine anything of what he meant in the Middle Ages. And Victorian shopkeepers did not conceive themselves as taking part in any such romance as the adventure of Courtrai, where the mediæval shop-keepers more than won their spurs—for they won the spurs of their enemies.

I have a very simple motive and excuse for telling the little I know of this true tale. I have met in my wanderings a man brought up in the lower quarters of a great house, fed mainly on its leavings and burdened mostly with its labours. I know that his complaints are stilled, and his status justified, by a story that is told to him. It is about how his grandfather was a chimpanzee and his father a wild man of the woods, caught by hunters and tamed into something like intelligence. In the light of this, he may well be thankful for the almost human life that he enjoys; and may be content with the hope of leaving behind him a yet more evolved animal. Strangely enough, the calling of this story by the sacred name of Progress ceased to satisfy me when I began to suspect (and to discover) that it is not true. I know by now enough at least of his origin to know that he was not evolved, but simply disinherited. His family tree is not a monkey tree, save in the sense that no monkey could have climbed it; rather it is like that tree torn up by the roots and named "Dedischado," on the shield of the unknown knight.

2. THE PROVINCE OF BRITAIN

The land on which we live once had the highly poetic privilege of being the end of the world. Its extremity was *ultima Thule*, the other end of nowhere. When these islands, lost in a night of northern seas, were lit up at last by the long searchlights of Rome, it was felt that the remotest remnant of things had been touched; and more for pride than possession.

The sentiment was not unsuitable, even in geography. About these realms upon the edge of everything there was really something that can only be called edgy. Britain is not so much an island as an archipelago; it is at least a labyrinth of peninsulas. In few of the kindred countries can one so easily and so strangely find sea in the fields or fields in the sea. The great rivers seem not only to meet in the ocean, but barely to miss each other in the hills: the whole land, though low as a whole, leans towards the west in shouldering mountains; and a prehistoric tradition has taught it to look towards the sunset for islands yet dreamier than its own. The islanders are of a kind with their islands. Different as are the nations into which they are now divided, the Scots, the English, the Irish, the Welsh of the western uplands, have something altogether different from the humdrum docility of the inland Germans, or from the *bon sens français* which can be at will trenchant or trite. There is something common to all the Britons, which even Acts of Union have not torn asunder. The nearest name for it is insecurity, something fitting in men walking on cliffs and the verge of things. Adventure, a lonely taste in liberty, a humour without wit, perplex their critics and perplex themselves. Their souls are fretted like their coasts. They have an embarrassment, noted by all foreigners: it is expressed, perhaps, in the Irish by a confusion of speech and in the English by a confusion of thought. For the Irish bull is a license with the symbol of language. But Bull's own bull, the English bull, is "a dumb ox of thought"; a standing mystification in the mind. There is something double in the thoughts as of the soul mirrored in many waters. Of all peoples they are least attached to the purely classical; the imperial plainness which the French do finely and the Germans coarsely, but the Britons hardly at all. They are constantly colonists and emigrants; they have the name of being at home in every country. But they are in exile in their own country. They are torn between love of home and love of something else; of which the sea may be the explanation or may be only the symbol. It is also found in a nameless nursery rhyme which is the finest line in English literature and the dumb refrain of all English poems—"Over the hills and far away."

The great rationalist hero who first conquered Britain, whether or no he was the detached demigod of "Cæsar and Cleopatra," was certainly a Latin of the Latins, and described these islands when he found them with all the curt positivism of his pen of steel. But even Julius Cæsar's brief account of the Britons leaves on us something of this mystery, which is more than ignorance of fact. They were apparently ruled by that terrible thing, a pagan priesthood. Stones now shapeless yet arranged in symbolic shapes bear witness to the order and labour of those that lifted them. Their worship was probably Nature-worship; and while such a basis may count for something in the elemental quality that has always soaked the island arts, the collision between it and the tolerant Empire suggests the presence of something which generally grows out of Nature-worship—I mean the unnatural. But upon nearly all the matters of modern controversy Cæsar is silent. He is silent about whether the language was "Celtic"; and some of the place-names have even given rise to a suggestion that, in parts at least, it was already Teutonic. I am not capable of pronouncing upon the truth of such speculations, but I am of pronouncing upon their importance; at least, to my own very simple purpose. And indeed their importance has been very much exaggerated. Cæsar professed to give no more than the glimpse of a traveller; but when, some considerable time after, the Romans returned and turned Britain into a Roman province, they continued to display a singular indifference to questions that have excited so many professors. What they cared about was getting and giving in Britain what they had got and given in Gaul. We do not know whether the Britons then, or for that matter the Britons now, were Iberian or Cymric or Teutonic. We do know that in a short time they were Roman.

Every now and then there is discovered in modern England some fragment such as a Roman pavement. Such Roman antiquities rather diminish than increase the Roman reality. They make something seem distant which is still very near, and something seem dead that is still alive. It is like writing a man's epitaph on his front door. The epitaph would probably be a compliment, but hardly a personal introduction. The important thing about France and England is not that they have Roman remains. They are Roman remains. In truth they are not so much remains as relics; for they are still working miracles. A row of poplars is a more Roman relic than a row of pillars. Nearly all that we call the works of nature have but grown like fungoids upon this original work of man; and our woods are mosses on the bones of a giant. Under the seed of our harvests and the roots of our trees is a foundation of which the fragments of tile and brick are but emblems; and under the colours of our wildest flowers are the colours of a Roman pavement.

Britain was directly Roman for fully four hundred years; longer than she has been Protestant, and very much longer than she has been industrial. What was meant by being Roman it is necessary in a few lines to say, or no sense can be made of what happened after, especially of what happened immediately after. Being Roman did *not* mean being subject, in the sense that one savage tribe will enslave another, or in the sense that the cynical politicians of recent times watched with a horrible hopefulness for the evanescence of the Irish. Both conquerors and conquered were heathen, and both had the institutions which seem to us to give an inhumanity to heathenism: the triumph, the slave-market, the lack of all the sensitive nationalism of modern history. But the Roman Empire did not destroy nations; if anything, it created them. Britons were not originally proud of being Britons; but they were proud of being Romans. The Roman steel was at least as much a magnet as a sword. In truth it was rather a round mirror of steel, in which every people came to see itself. For Rome as Rome the very smallness of the civic origin was a warrant for the largeness of the civic experiment. Rome itself obviously could not rule the world, any more than Rutland. I mean it could not rule the other races as the Spartans ruled the Helots or the Americans ruled the negroes. A machine so huge had to be human; it had to have a handle that fitted any man's hand. The Roman Empire necessarily became less Roman as it became more of an Empire; until not very long after Rome gave conquerors to Britain, Britain was giving emperors to Rome. Out of Britain, as the Britons boasted, came at length the great Empress Helena, who was the mother of Constantine. And it was Constantine, as all men know, who first nailed up that proclamation which all after generations have in truth been struggling either to protect or to tear down.

About that revolution no man has ever been able to be impartial. The present writer will make no idle pretence of being so. That it was the most revolutionary of all revolutions, since it identified the dead body on a servile gibbet with the fatherhood in the skies, has long been a commonplace without ceasing to be a paradox. But there is another historic element that must also be realized. Without saying anything more of its tremendous essence, it is very necessary to note why even pre-Christian Rome was regarded as something mystical for long afterwards by all European men. The extreme view of it was held, perhaps, by Dante; but it pervaded mediævalism, and therefore still haunts modernity. Rome was regarded as Man, mighty, though fallen, because it was the utmost that Man had done. It was divinely necessary that the Roman Empire should succeed—if only that it might fail. Hence the school of Dante implied the paradox that the Roman soldiers killed Christ, not only by right, but even by divine right. That mere law might fail at its highest test it had to be real law, and not mere military lawlessness. Therefore God worked by Pilate as by Peter. Therefore the mediæval poet is eager to show that Roman government was simply good government, and not a usurpation. For it was the whole point of the Christian revolution to maintain that in this, good government was as bad as bad. Even good govern-

5

ment was not good enough to know God among the thieves. This is not only generally important as involving a colossal change in the conscience; the loss of the whole heathen repose in the complete sufficiency of the city or the state. It made a sort of eternal rule enclosing an eternal rebellion. It must be incessantly remembered through the first half of English history; for it is the whole meaning in the quarrel of the priests and kings.

The double rule of the civilization and the religion in one sense remained for centuries; and before its first misfortunes came it must be conceived as substantially the same everywhere. And however it began it largely ended in equality. Slavery certainly existed, as it had in the most democratic states of ancient times. Harsh officialism certainly existed, as it exists in the most democratic states of modern times. But there was nothing of what we mean in modern times by aristocracy, still less of what we mean by racial domination. In so far as any change was passing over that society with its two levels of equal citizens and equal slaves, it was only the slow growth of the power of the Church at the expense of the power of the Empire. Now it is important to grasp that the great exception to equality, the institution of Slavery, was slowly modified by both causes. It was weakened both by the weakening of the Empire and by the strengthening of the Church.

Slavery was for the Church not a difficulty of doctrine, but a strain on the imagination. Aristotle and the pagan sages who had defined the servile or "useful" arts, had regarded the slave as a tool, an axe to cut wood or whatever wanted cutting. The Church did not denounce the cutting; but she felt as if she was cutting glass with a diamond. She was haunted by the memory that the diamond is so much more precious than the glass. So Christianity could not settle down into the pagan simplicity that the man was made for the work, when the work was so much less immortally momentous than the man. At about this stage of a history of England there is generally told the anecdote of a pun of Gregory the Great; and this is perhaps the true point of it. By the Roman theory the barbarian bondmen were meant to be useful. The saint's mysticism was moved at finding them ornamental; and "Non Angli sed Angeli" meant more nearly "Not slaves, but souls." It is to the point, in passing, to note that in the modern country most collectively Christian, Russia, the serfs were always referred to as "souls." The great Pope's phrase, hackneyed as it is, is perhaps the first glimpse of the golden halos in the best Christian Art. Thus the Church, with whatever other faults, worked of her own nature towards greater social equality; and it is a historical error to suppose that the Church hierarchy worked with aristocracies, or was of a kind with them. It was an inversion of aristocracy; in the ideal of it, at least, the last were to be first. The Irish bull that "One man is as good as another and a great deal better" contains a truth, like many contradictions; a truth that was the link between Christianity and citizenship. Alone of all superiors, the saint does not depress the human dignity of others. He is not conscious of his superiority to them; but only more conscious of his inferiority than they are.

But while a million little priests and monks like mice were already nibbling at the bonds of the ancient servitude, another process was going on, which has here been called the weakening of the Empire. It is a process which is to this day very difficult to explain. But it affected all the institutions of all the provinces, especially the institution of Slavery. But of all the provinces its effect was heaviest in Britain, which lay on or beyond the borders. The case of Britain, however, cannot possibly be considered alone. The first half of English history has been made quite unmeaning in the schools by the attempt to tell it without reference to that corporate Christendom in which it took part and pride. I fully accept the truth in Mr. Kipling's question of "What can they know of England who only England know?" and merely differ from the view that they will best broaden their minds by the study of Wagga-Wagga and Timbuctoo. It is therefore necessary, though very difficult, to frame in few words some idea of what happened to the whole European race.

Rome itself, which had made all that strong world, was the weakest thing in it. The centre had been growing fainter and fainter, and now the centre disappeared. Rome had as much freed the world as ruled it, and now she could rule no more. Save for the presence of the Pope and his constantly increasing supernatural prestige, the eternal city became like one of her own provincial towns. A loose localism was the result rather than any conscious intellectual mutiny. There was anarchy, but there was no rebellion. For rebellion must have a principle, and therefore (for those who can think) an authority. Gibbon called his great pageant of prose "The Decline and Fall of the Roman Empire." The Empire did decline, but it did not fall. It remains to this hour.

By a process very much more indirect even than that of the Church, this decentralization and drift also worked against the slave-state of antiquity. The localism did indeed produce that choice of territorial chieftains which came to be called Feudalism, and of which we shall speak later. But the direct possession of man by man the same localism tended to destroy; though this negative influence upon it bears no kind of proportion to the positive influence of the Catholic Church. The later pagan slavery, like our own industrial labour which increasingly resembles it, was worked on a larger and larger scale; and it was at last too large to control. The bondman found the visible Lord more distant than the new invisible one. The slave became the serf; that is, he could be shut in, but not shut out. When once he belonged to the land, it could not be long before the land belonged to him. Even in the old and rather fictitious language of chattel slavery, there is here a difference. It is the difference between a man being a chair and a man being a house. Canute might call for his throne; but if he wanted his throne-room he must go and get it himself. Similarly, he could tell his slave to run, but he could only tell his serf to stay. Thus the two slow changes of the time both tended to transform the tool into a man. His status began to have roots; and whatever has roots will have rights.

What the decline did involve everywhere was decivilization; the loss of letters, of laws, of roads and means of communication, the exaggeration of local colour into caprice. But on the edges of the Empire this decivilization became a definite barbarism, owing to the nearness of wild neighbours who were ready to destroy as deafly and blindly as things are destroyed by fire. Save for the lurid and apocalyptic locust-flight of the Huns, it is perhaps an exaggeration to talk, even in those darkest ages, of a deluge of the barbarians; at least when we are speaking of the old civilization as a whole. But a deluge of barbarians is not entirely an exaggeration of what happened on some of the borders of the Empire; of such edges of the known world as we began by describing in these pages. And on the extreme edge of the world lay Britain.

It may be true, though there is little proof of it, that the Roman civilization itself was thinner in Britain than in the other provinces; but it was a very civilized civilization. It gathered round the great cities like York and Chester and London; for the cities are older than the counties, and indeed older even than the countries. These were connected by a skeleton of great roads which were and are the bones of Britain. But with the weakening of Rome the bones began to break under barbarian pressure, coming at first from the north; from the Picts who lay beyond Agricola's boundary in what is now the Scotch Lowlands. The whole of this bewildering time is full of temporary tribal alliances, generally mercenary; of barbarians paid to come on or barbarians paid to go away. It seems certain that in this welter Roman Britain bought help from ruder races living about that neck of Denmark where is now the duchy of Schleswig. Having been chosen only to fight somebody they naturally fought anybody; and a century of fighting followed, under the trampling of which the Roman pavement was broken into yet smaller pieces. It is perhaps permissible to disagree with the historian Green when he says that no spot should be more sacred to modern Englishmen than the neighbourhood of Ramsgate, where the Schleswig people are supposed to have landed; or when he suggests that their appearance is the real beginning of our island story. It would be rather more true to say that it was nearly, though prematurely, the end of it.

3. THE AGE OF LEGENDS

We should be startled if we were quietly reading a prosaic modern novel, and somewhere in the middle it turned without warning into a fairy tale. We should be surprised if one of the spinsters in *Cranford*, after tidily sweeping the room with a broom, were to fly away on a broomstick. Our attention would be arrested if one of Jane Austen's young ladies who had just met a dragoon were to walk a little further and meet a dragon. Yet something very like this extraordinary transition takes place in British history at the end of the purely Roman period. We have to do with rational and almost mechanical accounts of encampment and engineering, of a busy bureaucracy and occasional frontier wars, quite modern in their efficiency and inefficiency;

and then all of a sudden we are reading of wandering bells and wizard lances, of wars against men as tall as trees or as short as toadstools. The soldier of civilization is no longer fighting with Goths but with goblins; the land becomes a labyrinth of faërie towns unknown to history; and scholars can suggest but cannot explain how a Roman ruler or a Welsh chieftain towers up in the twilight as the awful and unbegotten Arthur. The scientific age comes first and the mythological age after it. One working example, the echoes of which lingered till very late in English literature, may serve to sum up the contrast. The British state which was found by Cæsar was long believed to have been founded by Brutus. The contrast between the one very dry discovery and the other very fantastic foundation has something decidedly comic about it; as if Cæsar's "Et tu, Brute," might be translated, "What, *you* here?" But in one respect the fable is quite as important as the fact. They both testify to the reality of the Roman foundation of our insular society, and show that even the stories that seem prehistoric are seldom pre-Roman. When England is Elfland, the elves are not the Angles. All the phrases that can be used as clues through that tangle of traditions are more or less Latin phrases. And in all our speech there was no word more Roman than "romance."

The Roman legions left Britain in the fourth century. This did not mean that the Roman civilization left it; but it did mean that the civilization lay far more open both to admixture and attack. Christianity had almost certainly come to Britain, not indeed otherwise than by the routes established by Rome, but certainly long before the official Roman mission of Gregory the Great. It had certainly been largely swamped by later heathen invasions of the undefended coasts. It may then rationally be urged that the hold both of the Empire and its new religion were here weaker than elsewhere, and that the description of the general civilization in the last chapter is proportionately irrelevant. This, however, is not the chief truth of the matter.

There is one fundamental fact which must be understood of the whole of this period. Yet a modern man must very nearly turn his mind upside down to understand it. Almost every modern man has in his head an association between freedom and the future. The whole culture of our time has been full of the notion of "A Good Time Coming." Now the whole culture of the Dark Ages was full of the notion of "A Good Time Going." They looked backwards to old enlightenment and forwards to new prejudices. In our time there has come a quarrel between faith and hope—which perhaps must be healed by charity. But they were situated otherwise. They hoped—but it may be said that they hoped for yesterday. All the motives that make a man a progressive now made a man a conservative then. The more he could keep of the past the more he had of a fair law and a free state; the more he gave way to the future the more he must endure of ignorance and privilege. All we call reason was one with all we call reaction. And this is the clue which we must carry with us through the lives of all the great men of the Dark Ages; of Alfred, of Bede, of Dunstan. If the most extreme modern Republican were put back in that period he would be an equally extreme Papist or even Imperialist.

For the Pope was what was left of the Empire; and the Empire what was left of the Republic.

We may compare the man of that time, therefore, to one who has left free cities and even free fields behind him, and is forced to advance towards a forest. And the forest is the fittest metaphor, not only because it was really that wild European growth cloven here and there by the Roman roads, but also because there has always been associated with forests another idea which increased as the Roman order decayed. The idea of the forests was the idea of enchantment. There was a notion of things being double or different from themselves, of beasts behaving like men and not merely, as modern wits would say, of men behaving like beasts. But it is precisely here that it is most necessary to remember that an age of reason had preceded the age of magic. The central pillar which has sustained the storied house of our imagination ever since has been the idea of the civilized knight amid the savage enchantments; the adventures of a man still sane in a world gone mad.

The next thing to note in the matter is this: that in this barbaric time none of the *heroes* are barbaric. They are only heroes if they are anti-barbaric. Men real or mythical, or more probably both, became omnipresent like gods among the people, and forced themselves into the faintest memory and the shortest record, exactly in proportion as they had mastered the heathen madness of the time and preserved the Christian rationality that had come from Rome. Arthur has his name because he killed the heathen; the heathen who killed him have no names at all. Englishmen who know nothing of English history, but less than nothing of Irish history, have heard somehow or other of Brian Boru, though they spell it Boroo and seem to be under the impression that it is a joke. It is a joke the subtlety of which they would never have been able to enjoy, if King Brian had not broken the heathen in Ireland at the great Battle of Clontarf. The ordinary English reader would never have heard of Olaf of Norway if he had not "preached the Gospel with his sword"; or of the Cid if he had not fought against the Crescent. And though Alfred the Great seems to have deserved his title even as a personality, he was not so great as the work he had to do.

But the paradox remains that Arthur is more real than Alfred. For the age is the age of legends. Towards these legends most men adopt by instinct a sane attitude; and, of the two, credulity is certainly much more sane than incredulity. It does not much matter whether most of the stories are true; and (as in such cases as Bacon and Shakespeare) to realize that the question does not matter is the first step towards answering it correctly. But before the reader dismisses anything like an attempt to tell the earlier history of the country by its legends, he will do well to keep two principles in mind, both of them tending to correct the crude and very thoughtless scepticism which has made this part of the story so sterile. The nineteenth-century historians went on the curious principle of dismissing all people of whom tales are told, and concentrating upon people of whom nothing is told. Thus, Arthur is made utterly impersonal because all legends are lies, but somebody of the type of Hengist is made quite an important personality, merely because nobody thought him important enough to lie about. Now this is to reverse all common sense. A great many witty sayings are attributed to Talleyrand which were really said by somebody else. But they would not be so attributed if Talleyrand had been a fool, still less if he had been a fable. That fictitious stories are told about a person is, nine times out of ten, extremely good evidence that there was somebody to tell them about. Indeed some allow that marvellous things were done, and that there may have been a man named Arthur at the time in which they were done; but here, so far as I am concerned, the distinction becomes rather dim. I do not understand the attitude which holds that there was an Ark and a man named Noah, but cannot believe in the existence of Noah's Ark.

The other fact to be remembered is that scientific research for the last few years has worked steadily in the direction of confirming and not dissipating the legends of the populace. To take only the obvious instance, modern excavators with modern spades have found a solid stone labyrinth in Crete, like that associated with the Minataur, which was conceived as being as cloudy a fable as the Chimera. To most people this would have seemed quite as frantic as finding the roots of Jack's Beanstalk or the skeletons in Bluebeard's cupboard, yet it is simply the fact. Finally, a truth is to be remembered which scarcely ever is remembered in estimating the past. It is the paradox that the past is always present: yet it is not what was, but whatever seems to have been; for all the past is a part of faith. What did they believe of their fathers? In this matter new discoveries are useless because they are new. We may find men wrong in what they thought they were, but we cannot find them wrong in what they thought they thought. It is therefore very practical to put in a few words, if possible, something of what a man of these islands in the Dark Ages would have said about his ancestors and his inheritance. I will attempt here to put some of the simpler things in their order of importance as he would have seen them; and if we are to understand our fathers who first made this country anything like itself, it is most important that we should remember that if this was not their real past, it was their real memory.

After that blessed crime, as the wit of mystics called it, which was for these men hardly second to the creation of the world, St. Joseph of Arimathea, one of the few followers of the new religion who seem to have been wealthy, set sail as a missionary, and after long voyages came to that litter of little islands which seemed to the men of the Mediterranean something like the last clouds of the sunset. He came up upon the western and wilder side of that wild and western land, and made his way to a valley which through all the oldest records is called Avalon. Something of rich rains and warmth in its westland meadows, or something in some lost pagan traditions about it, made it persistently regarded as a kind of Earthly Paradise. Arthur, after being slain at Lyonesse, is carried here, as if to heaven. Here the pilgrim planted his staff in the soil; and it took root as a tree that blossoms on Christmas Day.

A mystical materialism marked Christianity from its birth; the very soul of it was a body. Among the stoical philosophies and oriental negations that were its first foes it fought fiercely and particularly for a supernatural freedom to cure concrete maladies by concrete substances. Hence the scattering of relics was everywhere like the scattering of seed. All who took their mission from the divine tragedy bore tangible fragments which became the germs of churches and cities. St. Joseph carried the cup which held the wine of the Last Supper and the blood of the Crucifixion to that shrine in Avalon which we now call Glastonbury; and it became the heart of a whole universe of legends and romances, not only for Britain but for Europe. Throughout this tremendous and branching tradition it is called the Holy Grail. The vision of it was especially the reward of that ring of powerful paladins whom King Arthur feasted at a Round Table, a symbol of heroic comradeship such as was afterwards imitated or invented by mediæval knighthood. Both the cup and the table are of vast importance emblematically in the psychology of the chivalric experiment. The idea of a round table is not merely universality but equality. It has in it, modified of course, by other tendencies to differentiation, the same idea that exists in the very word "peers," as given to the knights of Charlemagne. In this the Round Table is as Roman as the round arch, which might also serve as a type; for instead of being one barbaric rock merely rolled on the others, the king was rather the keystone of an arch. But to this tradition of a level of dignity was added something unearthly that was from Rome, but not of it; the privilege that inverted all privileges; the glimpse of heaven which seemed almost as capricious as fairyland; the flying chalice which was veiled from the highest of all the heroes, and which appeared to one knight who was hardly more than a child.

Rightly or wrongly, this romance established Britain for after centuries as a country with a chivalrous past. Britain had been a mirror of universal knighthood. This fact, or fancy, is of colossal import in all ensuing affairs, especially the affairs of barbarians. These and numberless other local legends are indeed for us buried by the forests of popular fancies that have grown out of them. It is all the harder for the serious modern mind because our fathers felt at home with these tales, and therefore took liberties with them. Probably the rhyme which runs,

> "When good King Arthur ruled this land
> He was a noble king,
> He stole three pecks of barley meal,"

is much nearer the true mediæval note than the aristocratic stateliness of Tennyson. But about all these grotesques of the popular fancy there is one last thing to be remembered. It must especially be remembered by those who would dwell exclusively on documents, and take no note of tradition at all. Wild as would be the results of credulity concerning all the old wives' tales, it would not be so wild as the errors that can arise from trusting to written evidence when there is not enough of it. Now the whole written evidence for the first parts of our history would go into a small book. A very few details are mentioned, and none are explained. A fact thus standing alone, without the key of contemporary thought, may be very much more misleading than any fable. To know what word an archaic scribe wrote without being sure of what thing he meant, may produce a result that is literally mad. Thus, for instance, it would be unwise to accept literally the tale that St. Helena was not only a native of Colchester, but was a daughter of Old King Cole. But it would not be very unwise; not so unwise as some things that are deduced from documents. The natives of Colchester certainly did honour to St. Helena, and might have had a king named Cole. According to the more serious story, the saint's father was an innkeeper; and the only recorded action of Cole is well within the resources of that calling. It would not be nearly so unwise as to deduce from the written word, as some critic of the future may do, that the natives of Colchester were oysters.

4. THE DEFEAT OF THE BARBARIANS

It is a quaint accident that we employ the word "short-sighted" as a condemnation; but not the word "long-sighted," which we should probably use, if at all, as a compliment. Yet the one is as much a malady of vision as the other. We rightly say, in rebuke of a small-minded modernity, that it is very short-sighted to be indifferent to all that is historic. But it is as disastrously long-sighted to be interested only in what is prehistoric. And this disaster has befallen a large proportion of the learned who grope in the darkness of unrecorded epochs for the roots of their favourite race or races. The wars, the enslavements, the primitive marriage customs, the colossal migrations and massacres upon which their theories repose, are no part of history or even of legend. And rather than trust with entire simplicity to these it would be infinitely wiser to trust to legend of the loosest and most local sort. In any case, it is as well to record even so simple a conclusion as that what is prehistoric is unhistorical.

But there is another way in which common sense can be brought to the criticism of some prodigious racial theories. To employ the same figure, suppose the scientific historians explain the historic centuries in terms of a prehistoric division between short-sighted and long-sighted men. They could cite their instances and illustrations. They would certainly explain the curiosity of language I mentioned first, as showing that the short-sighted were the conquered race, and their name therefore a term of contempt. They could give us very graphic pictures of the rude tribal war. They could show how the long-sighted people were always cut to pieces in hand-to-hand struggles with axe and knife; until, with the invention of bows and arrows, the advantage veered to the long-sighted, and their enemies were shot down in droves. I could easily write a ruthless romance about it, and still more easily a ruthless anthropological theory. According to that thesis which refers all moral to material changes, they could explain the tradition that old people grow conservative in politics by the well-known fact that old people grow more long-sighted. But I think there might be one thing about this theory which would stump us, and might even, if it be possible, stump them. Suppose it were pointed out that through all the three thousand years of recorded history, abounding in literature of every conceivable kind, there was not so much as a mention of the oculist question for which all had been dared and done. Suppose not one of the living or dead languages of mankind had so much as a word for "long-sighted" or "short-sighted." Suppose, in short, the question that had torn the whole world in two was never even asked at all, until some spectacle-maker suggested it somewhere about 1750. In that case I think we should find it hard to believe that this physical difference had really played so fundamental a part in human history. And that is exactly the case with the physical difference between the Celts, the Teutons and the Latins.

I know of no way in which fair-haired people can be prevented from falling in love with dark-haired people; and I do not believe that whether a man was long-headed or round-headed ever made much difference to any one who felt inclined to break his head. To all mortal appearance, in all mortal records and experience, people seem to have killed or spared, married or refrained from marriage, made kings or made slaves, with reference to almost any other consideration except this one. There was the love of a valley or a village, a site or a family; there were enthusiasms for a prince and his hereditary office; there were passions rooted in locality, special emotions about sea-folk or mountain-folk; there were historic memories of a cause or an alliance; there was, more than all, the tremendous test of religion. But of a cause like that of the Celts or Teutons, covering half the earth, there was little or nothing. Race was not only never at any given moment a motive, but it was never even an excuse. The Teutons never had a creed; they never had a cause; and it was only a few years ago that they began even to have a cant.

The orthodox modern historian, notably Green, remarks on the singularity of Britain in being alone of all Roman provinces wholly cleared and repeopled by a Germanic race. He does not entertain, as an escape from the singularity of this event, the possibility that it never happened. In the same spirit he deals with the little that can be quoted of the Teutonic society. His ideal picture of it is completed in small touches which even an amateur can detect as dubious. Thus he will touch on the Teuton with a phrase like "the basis of their society was the free man"; and on the Roman with a phrase like "the mines, if worked by forced labour, must have been a source of endless oppression." The simple fact being that the Roman and the Teuton both had slaves, he treats the Teuton free man as the only thing to be considered, not only then but now; and then goes out of his way to say that if the Roman treated his slaves badly, the slaves were badly treated. He expresses a "strange disappointment" that Gildas, the only British chronicler, does not describe the great Teutonic system. In the opinion of Gildas, a modification of that of Gregory, it was a case of *non Angli sed diaboli*. The modern Teutonist is "disappointed" that the contemporary authority saw nothing in his Teutons except wolves, dogs, and whelps from the kennel of barbarism. But it is at least faintly tenable that there was nothing else to be seen.

In any case when St. Augustine came to the largely barbarized land, with what may be called the second of the three great southern visitations which civilized these islands, he did not see any ethnological problems, whatever there may have been to be seen. With him or his converts the chain of literary testimony is taken up again; and we must look at the world as they saw it. He found a king ruling in Kent, beyond whose borders lay other kingdoms of about the same size, the kings of which were all apparently heathen. The names of these kings were mostly what we call Teutonic names; but those who write the almost entirely hagiological records did not say, and apparently did not ask, whether the populations were in this sense of unmixed blood. It is at least possible that, as on the Continent, the kings and courts were almost the only Teutonic element. The Christians found converts, they found patrons, they found persecutors; but they did not find Ancient Britons because they did not look for them; and if they moved among pure Anglo-Saxons they had not the gratification of knowing it. There was, indeed, what all history attests, a marked change of feeling towards the marches of Wales. But all history also attests that this is always found, apart from any difference in race, in the transition from the lowlands to the mountain country. But of all the things they found the thing that counts most in English history is this: that some of the kingdoms at least did correspond to genuine human divisions, which not only existed then but which exist now. Northumbria is still a truer thing than Northumberland. Sussex is still Sussex; Essex is still Essex. And that third Saxon kingdom whose name is not even to be found upon the map, the kingdom of Wessex, is called the West Country and is to-day the most real of them all.

The last of the heathen kingdoms to accept the cross was Mercia, which corresponds very roughly to what we call the Midlands. The unbaptized king, Penda, has even achieved a certain picturesqueness through this fact, and through the forays and furious ambitions which constituted the rest of his reputation; so much so that the other day one of those mystics who will believe anything but Christianity proposed to "continue the work of Penda" in Ealing: fortunately not on any large scale. What that prince believed or disbelieved it is now impossible and perhaps unnecessary to discover; but this last stand of his central kingdom is not insignificant. The isolation of the Mercian was perhaps due to the fact that Christianity grew from the eastern and western coasts. The eastern growth was, of course, the Augustinian mission, which had already made Canterbury the spiritual capital of the island. The western grew from whatever was left of the British Christianity. The two clashed, not in creed but in customs; and the Augustinians ultimately prevailed. But the work from the west had already been enormous. It is possible that some prestige went with the possession of Glastonbury, which was like a piece of the Holy Land; but behind Glastonbury there was an even grander and more impressive power. There irradiated to all Europe at that time the glory of the golden age of Ireland. There the Celts were the classics of Christian art, opened in the Book of Kels four hundred years before its time. There the baptism of the whole people had been a spontaneous popular festival which reads almost like a picnic; and thence came crowds of enthusiasts for the

Gospel almost literally like men running with good news. This must be remembered through the development of that dark dual destiny that has bound us to Ireland: for doubts have been thrown on a national unity which was not from the first a political unity. But if Ireland was not one kingdom it was in reality one bishopric. Ireland was not converted but created by Christianity, as a stone church is created; and all its elements were gathered as under a garment, under the genius of St. Patrick. It was the more individual because the religion was mere religion, without the secular conveniences. Ireland was never Roman, and it was always Romanist.

But indeed this is, in a lesser degree, true of our more immediate subject. It is the paradox of this time that only the unworldly things had any worldly success. The politics are a nightmare; the kings are unstable and the kingdoms shifting; and we are really never on solid ground except on consecrated ground. The material ambitions are not only always unfruitful but nearly always unfulfilled. The castles are all castles in the air; it is only the churches that are built on the ground. The visionaries are the only practical men, as in that extraordinary thing, the monastery, which was, in many ways, to be the key of our history. The time was to come when it was to be rooted out of our country with a curious and careful violence; and the modern English reader has therefore a very feeble idea of it and hence of the ages in which it worked. Even in these pages a word or two about its primary nature is therefore quite indispensable.

In the tremendous testament of our religion there are present certain ideals that seem wilder than impieties, which have in later times produced wild sects professing an almost inhuman perfection on certain points; as in the Quakers who renounce the right of self-defence, or the Communists who refuse any personal possessions. Rightly or wrongly, the Christian Church had from the first dealt with these visions as being special spiritual adventures which were to the adventurous. She reconciled them with natural human life by calling them specially good, without admitting that the neglect of them was necessarily bad. She took the view that it takes all sorts to make a world, even the religious world; and used the man who chose to go without arms, family, or property as a sort of exception that proved the rule. Now the interesting fact is that he really did prove it. This madman who would not mind his own business becomes the business man of the age. The very word "monk" is a revolution, for it means solitude and came to mean community—one might call it sociability. What happened was that this communal life became a sort of reserve and refuge behind the individual life; a hospital for every kind of hospitality. We shall see later how this same function of the common life was given to the common land. It is hard to find an image for it in individualist times; but in private life we most of us know the friend of the family who helps it by being outside, like a fairy godmother. It is not merely flippant to say that monks and nuns stood to mankind as a sort of sanctified league of aunts and uncles. It is a commonplace that they did everything that nobody else would do; that the abbeys kept the world's diary, faced the plagues of all flesh, taught the first technical arts, preserved the pagan literature, and above all, by a perpetual patchwork of charity, kept the poor from the most distant sight of their modern despair. We still find it necessary to have a reserve of philanthropists, but we trust it to men who have made themselves rich, not to men who have made themselves poor. Finally, the abbots and abbesses were elective. They introduced representative government, unknown to ancient democracy, and in itself a semi-sacramental idea. If we could look from the outside at our own institutions, we should see that the very notion of turning a thousand men into one large man walking to Westminster is not only an act or faith, but a fairy tale. The fruitful and effective history of Anglo-Saxon England would be almost entirely a history of its monasteries. Mile by mile, and almost man by man, they taught and enriched the land. And then, about the beginning of the ninth century, there came a turn, as of the twinkling of an eye, and it seemed that all their work was in vain.

That outer world of universal anarchy that lay beyond Christendom heaved another of its colossal and almost cosmic waves and swept everything away. Through all the eastern gates, left open, as it were, by the first barbarian auxiliaries, burst a plague of seafaring savages from Denmark and Scandinavia; and the recently baptized barbarians were again flooded by the unbaptized. All this time, it must be remembered, the actual central mechanism of Roman government had been running down like a clock. It was really a race between the driving energy of the missionaries on the edges of the Empire and the galloping paralysis of the city at the centre. In the ninth century the heart had stopped before the hands could bring help to it. All the monastic civilization which had grown up in Britain under a vague Roman protection perished unprotected. The toy kingdoms of the quarrelling Saxons were smashed like sticks; Guthrum, the pirate chief, slew St. Edmund, assumed the crown of East England, took tribute from the panic of Mercia, and towered in menace over Wessex, the last of the Christian lands. The story that follows, page after page, is only the story of its despair and its destruction. The story is a string of Christian defeats alternated with victories so vain as to be more desolate than defeats. It is only in one of these, the fine but fruitless victory at Ashdown, that we first see in the dim struggle, in a desperate and secondary part, the figure who has given his title to the ultimate turning of the tide. For the victor was not then the king, but only the king's younger brother. There is, from the first, something humble and even accidental about Alfred. He was a great understudy. The interest of his early life lies in this: that he combined an almost commonplace coolness, and readiness for the ceaseless small bargains and shifting combinations of all that period, with the flaming patience of saints in times of persecution. While he would dare anything for the faith, he would bargain in anything except the faith. He was a conqueror, with no ambition; an author only too glad to be a translator; a simple, concentrated, wary man, watching the fortunes of one thing, which he piloted both boldly and cautiously, and which he saved at last.

He had disappeared after what appeared to be the final heathen triumph and settlement, and is supposed to have lurked like an outlaw in a lonely islet in the impenetrable marshlands of the Parret; towards those wild western lands to which aboriginal races are held to have been driven by fate itself. But Alfred, as he himself wrote in words that are his challenge to the period, held that a Christian man was unconcerned with fate. He began once more to draw to him the bows and spears of the broken levies of the western shires, especially the men of Somerset; and in the spring of 878 he flung them at the lines before the fenced camp of the victorious Danes at Ethandune. His sudden assault was as successful as that at Ashdown, and it was followed by a siege which was successful in a different and very definite sense. Guthrum, the conqueror of England, and all his important supports, were here penned behind their palisades, and when at last they surrendered the Danish conquest had come to an end. Guthrum was baptized, and the Treaty of Wedmore secured the clearance of Wessex. The modern reader will smile at the baptism, and turn with greater interest to the terms of the treaty. In this acute attitude the modern reader will be vitally and hopelessly wrong. He must support the tedium of frequent references to the religious element in this part of English history, for without it there would never have been any English history at all. And nothing could clinch this truth more than the case of the Danes. In all the facts that followed, the baptism of Guthrum is really much more important than the Treaty of Wedmore. The treaty itself was a compromise, and even as such did not endure; a century afterwards a Danish king like Canute was really ruling in England. But though the Dane got the crown, he did not get rid of the cross. It was precisely Alfred's religious exaction that remained unalterable. And Canute himself is actually now only remembered by men as a witness to the futility of merely pagan power; as the king who put his own crown upon the image of Christ, and solemnly surrendered to heaven the Scandinavian empire of the sea.

5. ST. EDWARD AND THE NORMAN KINGS

The reader may be surprised at the disproportionate importance given to the name which stands first in the title of this chapter. I put it there as the best way of emphasizing, at the beginning of what we may call the practical part of our history, an elusive and rather strange thing. It can only be described as the strength of the weak kings.

It is sometimes valuable to have enough imagination to unlearn as well as to learn. I would ask the reader to forget his reading and everything that he learnt at school, and consider the English monarchy as it would then appear to him. Let him suppose that his acquaintance with the ancient kings has only come to him as it came to most men in simpler times, from nursery tales, from the names of places, from the dedications of churches and charities, from the tales in the tavern, and the tombs in the churchyard. Let us suppose such a person going upon some open and ordinary English way, such as the Thames valley to Windsor, or visiting some old seats of culture, such as Oxford or Cambridge. One of the first things, for instance, he would find would be Eton, a place transformed, indeed, by modern aristocracy, but still enjoying its mediæval wealth and remembering its mediæval origin. If he asked about that origin, it is probable that even a public schoolboy would know enough history to tell him that it was founded by Henry VI. If he went to Cambridge and looked with his own eyes for the college chapel which artistically towers above all others like a cathedral, he would probably ask about it, and be told it was King's College. If he asked which king, he would again be told Henry VI. If he then went into the library and looked up Henry VI. in an encyclopædia, he would find that the legendary giant, who had left these gigantic works behind him, was in history an almost invisible pigmy. Amid the varying and contending numbers of a great national quarrel, he is the only cipher. The contending factions carry him about like a bale of goods. His desires do not seem to be even ascertained, far less satisfied. And yet his real desires are satisfied in stone and marble, in oak and gold, and remain through all the maddest revolutions of modern England, while all the ambitions of those who dictated to him have gone away like dust upon the wind.

Edward the Confessor, like Henry VI., was not only an invalid but almost an idiot. It is said that he was wan like an albino, and that the awe men had of him was partly that which is felt for a monster of mental deficiency. His Christian charity was of the kind that borders on anarchism, and the stories about him recall the Christian fools in the great anarchic novels of Russia. Thus he is reported to have covered the retreat of a common thief upon the naked plea that the thief needed things more than he did. Such a story is in strange contrast to the claims made for other kings, that theft was impossible in their dominions. Yet the two types of king are afterwards praised by the same people; and the really arresting fact is that the incompetent king is praised the more highly of the two. And exactly as in the case of the last Lancastrian, we find that the praise has really a very practical meaning in the long run. When we turn from the destructive to the constructive side of the Middle Ages we find that the village idiot is the inspiration of cities and civic systems. We find his seal upon the sacred foundations of Westminster Abbey. We find the Norman victors in the hour of victory bowing before his very ghost. In the Tapestry of Bayeux, woven by Norman hands to justify the Norman cause and glorify the Norman triumph, nothing is claimed for the Conqueror beyond his conquest and the plain personal tale that excuses it, and the story abruptly ends with the breaking of the Saxon line at Battle. But over the bier of the decrepit zany, who died without striking a blow, over this and this alone, is shown a hand coming out of heaven, and declaring the true approval of the power that rules the world.

The Confessor, therefore, is a paradox in many ways, and in none more than in the false reputation of the "English" of that day. As I have indicated, there is some unreality in talking about the Anglo-Saxon at all. The Anglo-Saxon is a mythical and straddling giant, who has presumably left one footprint in England and the other in Saxony. But there was a community, or rather group of communities, living in Britain before the Conquest under what we call Saxon names, and of a blood probably more Germanic and certainly less French than the same communities after the Conquest. And they have a modern reputation which is exactly the reverse of their real one. The value of the Anglo-Saxon is exaggerated, and yet his virtues are ignored. Our Anglo-Saxon blood is supposed to be the practical part of us; but as a fact the Anglo-Saxons were more hopelessly unpractical than any Celt. Their racial influence is supposed to be healthy, or, what many think the same thing, heathen. But as a fact these "Teutons" were the mystics. The Anglo-Saxons did one thing, and one thing only, thoroughly well, as they were fitted to do it thoroughly well. They christened England. Indeed, they christened it before it was born. The one thing the Angles obviously and certainly could not manage to do was to become English. But they did become Christians, and indeed showed a particular disposition to become monks. Moderns who talk vaguely of them as our hardy ancestors never do justice to the real good they did us, by thus opening our history, as it were, with the fable of an age of innocence, and beginning all our chronicles, as so many chronicles began, with the golden initial of a saint. By becoming monks they served us in many very valuable and special capacities, but not notably, perhaps, in the capacity of ancestors.

Along the northern coast of France, where the Confessor had passed his early life, lay the lands of one of the most powerful of the French king's vassals, the Duke of Normandy. He and his people, who constitute one of the most picturesque and curious elements in European history, are confused for most of us by irrelevant controversies which would have been entirely unintelligible to them. The worst of these is the inane fiction which gives the name of Norman to the English aristocracy during its great period of the last three hundred years. Tennyson informed a lady of the name of Vere de Vere that simple faith was more valuable than Norman blood. But the historical student who can believe in Lady Clara as the possessor of the Norman blood must be himself a large possessor of the simple faith. As a matter of fact, as we shall see also when we come to the political scheme of the Normans, the notion is the negation of their real importance in history. The fashionable fancy misses what was best in the Normans, exactly as we have found it missing what was best in the Saxons. One does not know whether to thank the Normans more for appearing or for disappearing. Few philanthropists ever became so rapidly anonymous. It is the great glory of the Norman adventurer that he threw himself heartily into his chance position; and had faith not only in his comrades, but in his subjects, and even in his enemies. He was loyal to the kingdom he had not yet made. Thus the Norman Bruce becomes a Scot; thus the descendant of the Norman Strongbow becomes an Irishman. No men less than Normans can be conceived as remaining as a superior caste until the present time. But this alien and adventurous loyalty in the Norman, which appears in these other national histories, appears most strongly of all in the history we have here to follow. The Duke of Normandy does become a real King of England; his claim through the Confessor, his election by the Council, even his symbolic handfuls of the soil of Sussex, these are not altogether empty forms. And though both phrases would be inaccurate, it is very much nearer the truth to call William the first of the English than to call Harold the last of them.

An indeterminate debate touching the dim races that mixed without record in that dim epoch, has made much of the fact that the Norman edges of France, like the East Anglian edges of England, were deeply penetrated by the Norse invasions of the ninth century; and that the ducal house of Normandy, with what other families we know not, can be traced back to a Scandinavian seed. The unquestionable power of captaincy and creative legislation which belonged to the Normans, whoever they were, may be connected reasonably enough with some infusion of fresh blood. But if the racial theorists press the point to a comparison of races, it can obviously only be answered by a study of the two types in separation. And it must surely be manifest that more civilizing power has since been shown by the French when untouched by Scandinavian blood than by the Scandinavians when untouched by French blood. As much fighting (and more ruling) was done by the Crusaders who were never Vikings as by the Vikings who were never Crusaders. But in truth there is no need of such invidious analysis; we may willingly allow a real value to the Scandinavian contribution to the French as to the English nationality, so long as we firmly understand the ultimate historic fact that the duchy of Normandy was about as Scandinavian as the town of Norwich. But the debate has another danger, in that it tends to exaggerate even the personal importance of the Norman. Many as were his talents as a master, he is in history the servant of other and wider things. The landing of Lanfranc is perhaps more of a date than the landing of William. And Lanfranc was an Italian— like Julius Cæsar. The Norman is not in history a mere wall, the rather brutal boundary of a mere empire. The Norman is a gate. He is like one of those gates which still remain as he made them, with round arch and rude pattern and stout supporting columns; and what entered by that gate was civilization. William of Falaise has in history a title much higher than that of Duke of Normandy or King of England. He was what Julius Cæsar was, and what St. Augustine was: he was the ambassador of Europe to Britain.

William asserted that the Confessor, in the course of that connection which followed naturally from his Norman education, had promised the English crown to the holder of the Norman dukedom. Whether he did or not we shall probably never know: it is not intrinsically impossible or even improbable. To blame the promise as unpatriotic, even if it was given, is to read duties defined at a much later date into the first feudal chaos; to make such blame positive and personal is like expecting the Ancient Britons to sing "Rule Britannia." William further clinched his case by declaring that Harold, the principal Saxon noble and the most probable Saxon claimant, had, while enjoying the Duke's hospitality after a shipwreck, sworn upon sacred relics not to dispute the Duke's claim. About this episode also we must agree that we do not know; yet we shall be quite out of touch with the time if we say that we do not care. The element of sacrilege in the alleged perjury of Harold probably affected the Pope when he blessed a banner for William's army; but it did not affect the Pope much more than it would have affected the people; and Harold's people quite as much as William's. Harold's people presumably denied the fact; and their denial is probably the motive of the very marked and almost eager emphasis with which the Bayeux Tapestry asserts and reasserts the reality of the personal betrayal. There is here a rather arresting fact to be noted. A great part of this celebrated pictorial record is not concerned at all with the well-known historical events which we have only to note rapidly here. It does, indeed, dwell a little on the death of Edward; it depicts the difficulties of William's enterprise in the felling of forests for shipbuilding, in the crossing of the Channel, and especially in the charge up the hill at Hastings, in which full justice is done to the destructive resistance of Harold's army. But it was really after Duke William had disembarked and defeated Harold on the Sussex coast, that he did what is historically worthy to be called the Conquest. It is not until these later operations that we have the note of the new and scientific militarism from the Continent. Instead of marching upon London he marched round it; and crossing the Thames at Wallingford cut off the city from the rest of the country and compelled its surrender. He had himself elected king with all the forms that would have accompanied a peaceful succession to the Confessor, and after a brief return to Normandy took up the work of war again to bring all England under his crown. Marching through the snow, he laid waste the northern counties, seized Chester, and made rather than won a kingdom. These things are the foundations of historical England; but of these things the pictures woven in honour of his house tell us nothing. The Bayeux Tapestry may almost be said to stop before the Norman Conquest. But it tells in great detail the tale of some trivial raid into Brittany solely that Harold and William may appear as brothers in arms; and especially that William may be depicted in the very act of giving arms to Harold. And here again there is much more significance than a modern reader may fancy, in its bearing upon the new birth of that time and the ancient symbolism of arms. I have said that Duke William was a vassal of the King of France; and that phrase in its use and abuse is the key to the secular side of this epoch. William was indeed a most mutinous vassal, and a vein of such mutiny runs through his family fortunes: his sons Rufus and Henry I. disturbed him with internal ambitions antagonistic to his own. But it would be a blunder to allow such personal broils to obscure the system, which had indeed existed here before the Conquest, which clarified and confirmed it. That system we call Feudalism.

That Feudalism was the main mark of the Middle Ages is a commonplace of fashionable information; but it is of the sort that seeks the past rather in Wardour Street than Watling Street. For that matter, the very term "mediæval" is used for almost anything from Early English to Early Victorian. An eminent Socialist applied it to our armaments, which is like applying it to our aeroplanes. Similarly the just description of Feudalism, and of how far it was a part and how far rather an impediment in the main mediæval movement, is confused by current debates about quite modern things —especially that modern thing, the English squirearchy. Feudalism was very nearly the opposite of squirearchy. For it is the whole point of the squire that his ownership is absolute and is pacific. And it is the very definition of Feudalism that it was a tenure, and a tenure by military service. Men paid their rent in steel instead of gold, in spears and arrows against the enemies of their landlord. But even these landlords were not landlords in the modern sense; every one was practically as well as theoretically a tenant of the King; and even he often fell into a feudal inferiority to a Pope or an Emperor. To call it mere tenure by soldiering may seem a simplification; but indeed it is precisely here that it was not so simple as it seems. It is precisely a certain knot or enigma in the nature of Feudalism which makes half the struggle of European history, but especially English history.

There was a certain unique type of state and culture which we call mediæval, for want of a better word, which we see in the Gothic or the great Schoolmen. This thing in itself was above all things logical. Its very cult of authority was a thing of reason, as all men who can reason themselves instantly recognize, even if, like Huxley, they deny its premises or dislike its fruits. Being logical, it was very exact about who had the authority. Now Feudalism was not quite logical, and was never quite exact about who had the authority. Feudalism already flourished before the mediæval renascence began. It was, if not the forest the mediævals had to clear, at least the rude timber with which they had to build. Feudalism was a fighting growth of the Dark Ages before the Middle Ages; the age of barbarians resisted by semi-barbarians. I do not say this in disparagement of it. Feudalism was mostly a very human thing; the nearest contemporary name for it was homage, a word which almost means humanity. On the other hand, mediæval logic, never quite reconciled to it, could become in its extremes inhuman. It was often mere prejudice that protected men, and pure reason that burned them. The feudal units grew through the lively localism of the Dark Ages, when hills without roads shut in a valley like a garrison. Patriotism had to be parochial; for men had no country, but only a countryside. In such cases the lord grew larger than the king; but it bred not only a local lordship but a kind of local liberty. And it would be very inadvisable to ignore the freer element in Feudalism in English history. For it is the one kind of freedom that the English have had and held.

The knot in the system was something like this. In theory the King owned everything, like an earthly providence; and that made for despotism and "divine right," which meant in substance a natural authority. In one aspect the King was simply the one lord anointed by the Church, that is recognized by the ethics of the age. But while there was more royalty in theory, there could be more rebellion in practice. Fighting was much more equal than in our age of munitions, and the various groups could arm almost instantly with bows from the forest or spears from the smith. Where men are military there is no militarism. But it is more vital that while the kingdom was in this sense one territorial army, the regiments of it were also kingdoms. The sub-units were also sub-loyalties. Hence the loyalist to his lord might be a rebel to his king; or the king be a demagogue delivering him from the lord. This tangle is responsible for the tragic passions about betrayal, as in the case of William and Harold; the alleged traitor who is always found to be recurrent, yet always felt to be exceptional. To break the tie was at once easy and terrible. Treason in the sense of rebellion was then really felt as treason in the sense of treachery, since it was desertion on a perpetual battle-field. Now, there was even more of this civil war in English than in other history, and the more local and less logical energy on the whole prevailed. Whether there was something in those island idiosyncrasies, shapeless as sea-mists, with which this story began, or whether the Roman imprint had really been lighter than in Gaul, the feudal undergrowth prevented even a full attempt to build the *Civitas Dei*, or ideal mediæval state. What emerged was a compromise, which men long afterwards amused themselves by calling a constitution.

There are paradoxes permissible for the redressing of a bad balance in criticism, and which may safely even be emphasized so long as they are not isolated. One of these I have called at the beginning of this chapter the strength of the weak kings. And there is a complement of it, even in this crisis of the Norman mastery, which might well be called the weakness of the strong kings. William of Normandy succeeded immediately, he did not quite succeed ultimately; there was in his huge success a secret of failure that only bore fruit long after his death. It was certainly his single aim to simplify England into a popular autocracy, like that growing up in France; with that aim he scattered the feudal holdings in scraps, demanded a direct vow from the sub-vassals to himself, and used any tool against the barony, from the highest culture of the foreign ecclesiastics to the rudest relics of Saxon custom. But the very parallel of France makes the paradox startlingly apparent. It is a proverb that the first French kings were puppets; that the mayor of the palace was quite insolently the king of the king. Yet it is certain that the puppet became an idol; a popular idol of unparalleled power, before which all mayors and nobles bent or were broken. In France arose absolute government, the more because it was not precisely personal government. The King was already a thing—like the Republic. Indeed the mediæval Republics were rigid with divine right. In Norman England, perhaps, the government was too personal to be absolute. Anyhow, there is a real though recondite sense in which William the Conqueror was William the Conquered. When his two sons were dead, the whole country fell into a feudal chaos almost like that before the Conquest. In France the princes who had been slaves became something exceptional like priests; and one of them became a saint. But somehow our greatest kings were still barons; and by that very energy our barons became our kings.

6. THE AGE OF THE CRUSADES

The last chapter began, in an apparent irrelevance, with the name of St. Edward; and this one might very well begin with the name of St. George. His first appearance, it is said, as a patron of our people, occurred at the instance of Richard Cœur de Lion during his campaign in Palestine; and this, as we shall see, really stands for a new England which might well have a new saint. But the Confessor is a character in English history; whereas St. George, apart from his place in martyrology as a Roman soldier, can hardly be said to be a character in any history. And if we wish to understand the noblest and most neglected of human revolutions, we can hardly get closer to it than by considering this paradox, of how much progress and enlightenment was represented by thus passing from a chronicle to a romance.

In any intellectual corner of modernity can be found such a phrase as I have just read in a newspaper controversy: "Salvation, like other good things, must not come from outside." To call a spiritual thing external and not internal is the chief mode of modernist excommunication. But if our subject of study is mediæval and not modern, we must pit against this apparent platitude the very opposite idea. We must put ourselves in the posture of men who thought that almost every good thing came from outside—like good news. I confess that I am not impartial in my sympathies here; and that the newspaper phrase I quoted strikes me as a blunder about the very nature of life. I do not, in my private capacity, believe that a baby gets his best physical food by sucking his thumb; nor that a man gets his best moral food by sucking his soul, and denying its dependence on God or other good things. I would maintain that thanks are the highest form of thought; and that gratitude is happiness doubled by wonder. But this faith in receptiveness, and in respect for things outside oneself, need here do no more than help me in explaining what any version of this epoch ought in any case to explain. In nothing is the modern German more modern, or more mad, than in his dream of finding a German name for everything; eating his language, or in other words biting his tongue. And in nothing were the mediævals more free and sane than in their acceptance of names and emblems from outside their most beloved limits. The monastery would often not only take in the stranger but almost canonize him. A mere adventurer like Bruce was enthroned and thanked as if he had really come as a knight errant. And a passionately patriotic community more often than not had a foreigner for a patron saint. Thus crowds of saints were Irishmen, but St. Patrick was not an Irishman. Thus as the English gradually became a nation, they left the numberless Saxon saints in a sense behind them, passed over by comparison not only the sanctity of Edward but the solid fame of Alfred, and invoked a half mythical hero, striving in an eastern desert against an impossible monster.

That transition and that symbol stand for the Crusades. In their romance and reality they were the first English experience of learning, not only from the external, but the remote. England, like every Christian thing, had thriven on outer things without shame. From the roads of Cæsar to the churches of Lanfranc, it had sought its meat from God. But now the eagles were on the wing, scenting a more distant slaughter; they were seeking the strange things instead of receiving them. The English had stepped from acceptance to adventure, and the epic of their ships had begun. The scope of the great religious movement which swept England along with all the West would distend a book like this into huge disproportion, yet it would be much better to do so than to dismiss it in the distant and frigid fashion common in such short summaries. The inadequacy of our insular method in popular history is perfectly shown in the treatment of Richard Cœur de Lion. His tale is told with the implication that his departure for the Crusade was something like the escapade of a schoolboy running away to sea. It was, in this view, a pardonable or lovable prank; whereas in truth it was more like a responsible Englishman now going to the Front. Christendom was nearly one nation, and the Front was the Holy Land. That Richard himself was of an adventurous and even romantic temper is true, though it is not unreasonably romantic for a born soldier to do the work he does best. But the point of the argument against insular history is particularly illustrated here by the absence of a continental comparison. In this case we have only to step across the Straits of Dover to find the fallacy. Philip Augustus, Richard's contemporary in France, had the name of a particularly cautious and coldly public-spirited statesman; yet Philip Augustus went on the same Crusade. The reason was, of course, that the Crusades were, for all thoughtful Europeans, things of the highest statesmanship and the purest public spirit.

Some six hundred years after Christianity sprang up in the East and swept westwards, another great faith arose in almost the same eastern lands and followed it like its gigantic shadow. Like a shadow, it was at once a copy and a contrary. We call it Islam, or the creed of the Moslems; and perhaps its most explanatory description is that it was the final flaming up of the accumulated Orientalisms, perhaps of the accumulated Hebraisms, gradually rejected as the Church grew more European, or as Christianity turned into Christendom. Its highest motive was a hatred of idols, and in its view Incarnation was itself an idolatry. The two things it persecuted were the idea of God being made flesh and of His being afterwards made wood or stone. A study of the questions smouldering in the track of the prairie fire of the Christian conversion favours the suggestion that this fanaticism against art or mythology was at once a development and a reaction from that conversion, a sort of minority report of the Hebraists. In this sense Islam was something like a Christian heresy. The early heresies had been full of mad reversals and evasions of the Incarnation, rescuing their Jesus from the reality of his body even at the expense of the sincerity of his soul. And the Greek Iconoclasts had poured into Italy, breaking the popular statues and denouncing the idolatry of the Pope, until routed, in a style sufficiently symbolic, by the sword of the father of Charlemagne. It was all these disappointed negations that took fire from the genius of Mahomet, and launched out of the burning lands a cavalry charge that nearly conquered the world. And if it be suggested that a note on such Oriental origins is rather remote from a history of England, the answer is that this book may, alas! contain many digressions, but that this is not a digression. It is quite peculiarly necessary to keep in mind that this Semite god haunted Christianity like a ghost; to remember it in every European corner, but especially in our corner. If any one doubts the necessity, let him take a walk to all the parish churches in England within a radius of thirty miles, and ask why this stone virgin is headless or that coloured glass is gone. He will soon learn that it was lately, and in his own lanes and homesteads, that the ecstasy of the deserts returned, and his bleak northern island was filled with the fury of the Iconoclasts.

It was an element in this sublime and yet sinister simplicity of Islam that it knew no boundaries. Its very home was homeless. For it was born in a sandy waste among nomads, and it went everywhere because it came from nowhere. But in the Saracens of the early Middle Ages this nomadic quality in Islam was masked by a high civilization, more scientific if less creatively artistic than that of contemporary Christendom. The Moslem monotheism was, or appeared to be, the more rationalist religion of the two. This rootless refinement was characteristically advanced in abstract things, of which a memory remains in the very name of algebra. In comparison the Christian civilization was still largely instinctive, but its instincts were very strong and very much the other way. It was full of local affections, which found form in that system of *fences* which runs like a pattern through everything mediæval, from heraldry to the holding of land. There was a shape and colour in all their customs and statutes which can be seen in all their tabards and escutcheons; something at once strict and gay. This is not a departure from the interest in external things, but rather a part of it. The very welcome they would often give to a stranger from beyond the wall was a recognition of the wall. Those who think their own life all-sufficient do not see its limit as a wall, but as the end of the world. The Chinese called the white man "a sky-breaker." The mediæval spirit loved its part in life as a part, not a whole; its charter for it came from something else. There is a joke about a Benedictine monk who used the common grace of *Benedictus benedicat*, whereupon the unlettered Franciscan triumphantly retorted *Franciscus Franciscat*. It is something of a parable of mediæval history; for if there were a verb Franciscare it would be an approximate description of what St. Francis afterwards did. But that more individual mysticism was only approaching its birth, and *Benedictus benedicat* is very precisely the motto of the earliest mediævalism. I mean that everything is blessed from beyond, by something which has in its turn been blessed from beyond again; only the blessed bless. But the point which is the clue to the Crusades is this: that for them the beyond was not the infinite, as in a modern religion. Every beyond was a place. The mystery of locality, with all its hold on the human heart, was as much present in the most ethereal things of Christendom as it was absent from the most practical things of Islam. England would derive a thing from France, France from Italy, Italy from Greece, Greece from Palestine, Palestine from Paradise. It was not merely that a yeoman of Kent would have his house hallowed by the priest of the parish church, which was confirmed by Canterbury, which was confirmed by Rome. Rome herself did not worship herself, as in the pagan age. Rome herself looked eastward to the mysterious cradle of her creed, to a land of which the very earth was called holy. And when she looked eastward for it she saw the face of Mahound. She saw standing in the place that was her earthly heaven a devouring giant out of the deserts, to whom all places were the same.

It has been necessary thus to pause upon the inner emotions of the Crusade, because the modern English reader is widely cut off from these particular feelings of his fathers; and the real quarrel of Christendom and Islam, the fire-baptism of the young nations, could not otherwise be seized in its unique character. It was nothing so simple as a quarrel between two men who both wanted Jerusalem. It was the much deadlier quarrel between one man who wanted it and another man who could not see why it was wanted. The Moslem, of course, had his own holy places; but he has never felt about them as Westerns can feel about a field or a roof-tree; he thought of the holiness as holy, not of the places as places. The austerity which forbade him imagery, the wandering war that forbade him rest, shut him off from all that was breaking out and blossoming in our local patriotisms; just as it has given the Turks an empire without ever giving them a nation.

Now, the effect of this adventure against a mighty and mysterious enemy was simply enormous in the transformation of England, as of all the nations that were developing side by side with England. Firstly, we learnt enormously from what the Saracen did. Secondly, we learnt yet more enormously from what the Saracen did not do. Touching some of the good things which we lacked, we were fortunately able to follow him. But in all the good things which he lacked, we were confirmed like adamant to defy him. It may be said that Christians never knew how right they were till they went to war with Moslems. At once the most obvious and the most representative reaction was the reaction which produced the best of what we call Christian Art; and especially those grotesques of Gothic architecture, which are not only alive but kicking. The East as an environment, as an impersonal glamour, certainly stimulated the Western mind, but stimulated it rather to break the Moslem commandment than to keep it. It was as if the Christian were impelled, like a caricaturist, to cover all that faceless ornament with faces; to give heads to all those headless serpents and birds to all these lifeless trees. Statuary quickened and came to life under the veto of the enemy as under a benediction. The image, merely because it was called an idol, became not only an ensign but a weapon. A hundredfold host of stone sprang up all over the shrines and streets of Europe. The Iconoclasts made more statues than they destroyed.

The place of Cœur de Lion in popular fable and gossip is far more like his place in true history than the place of the mere denationalized ne'er-do-weel given him in our utilitarian school books. Indeed the vulgar rumour is nearly always much nearer the historical truth than the "educated" opinion of to-day; for tradition is truer than fashion. King Richard, as the typical Crusader, did make a momentous difference to England by gaining glory in the East, instead of devoting himself conscientiously to domestic politics in the exemplary manner of King John. The accident of his military genius and prestige gave England something which it kept for four hundred years, and without which it is incomprehensible throughout that period—the reputation of being in the very vanguard of chivalry. The great romances of the Round Table, the attachment of knighthood to the name of a British king, belong to this period. Richard was not only a knight but a troubadour; and culture and courtesy were linked up with the idea of English valour. The mediæval Englishman was even proud of being polite; which is at least no worse than being proud of money and bad manners, which is what many Englishmen in our later centuries have meant by their common sense.

Chivalry might be called the baptism of Feudalism. It was an attempt to bring the justice and even the logic of the Catholic creed into a military system which already existed; to turn its discipline into an initiation and its inequalities into a hierarchy. To the comparative grace of the new period belongs, of course, that considerable cultus of the dignity of woman, to which the word "chivalry" is often narrowed, or perhaps exalted. This also was a revolt against one of the worst gaps in the more polished civilization of the Saracens. Moslems denied even souls to women; perhaps from the same instinct which recoiled from the sacred birth, with its inevitable glorification of the mother; perhaps merely because, having originally had tents rather than houses, they had slaves rather than housewives. It is false to say that the chivalric view of women was merely an affectation, except in the sense in which there must always be an affectation where there is an ideal. It is the worst sort of superficiality not to see the pressure of a general sentiment merely because it is always broken up by events; the Crusade itself, for example, is more present and potent as a dream even than as a reality. From the first Plantagenet to the last Lancastrian it haunts the minds of English kings, giving as a background to their battles a mirage of Palestine. So a devotion like that of Edward I. to his queen was quite a real motive in the lives of multitudes of his contemporaries. When crowds of enlightened tourists, setting forth to sneer at the superstitions of the continent, are taking tickets and labelling luggage at the large railway station at the west end of the Strand, I do not know whether they all speak to their wives with a more flowing courtesy than their fathers in Edward's time, or whether they pause to meditate on the legend of a husband's sorrow, to be found in the very name of Charing Cross.

But it is a huge historical error to suppose that the Crusades concerned only that crust of society for which heraldry was an art and chivalry an etiquette. The direct contrary is the fact. The First Crusade especially was much more an unanimous popular rising than most that are called riots and revolutions. The Guilds, the great democratic systems of the time, often owed their increasing power to corporate fighting for the Cross; but I shall deal with such things later. Often it was not so much a levy of men as a trek of whole families, like new gipsies moving eastwards. And it has passed into a proverb that children by themselves often organized a crusade as they now organize a charade. But we shall best realize the fact by fancying every Crusade as a Children's Crusade. They were full of all that the modern world worships in children, because it has crushed it out of men. Their lives were full, as the rudest remains of their vulgarest arts are full, of something that we all saw out of the nursery window. It can best be seen later, for instance, in the lanced and latticed interiors of Memling, but it is ubiquitous in the older and more unconscious contemporary art; something that domesticated distant lands and made the horizon at home. They fitted into the corners of small houses the ends of the earth and the edges of the sky. Their perspective is rude and crazy, but it is perspective; it is not the decorative flatness of orientalism. In a word, their world, like a child's, is full of foreshortening, as of a short cut to fairyland. Their maps are more provocative than pictures. Their half-fabulous animals are monsters, and yet are pets. It is impossible to state verbally this very vivid atmosphere; but it was an atmosphere as well as an adventure. It was precisely these outlandish visions that truly came home to everybody; it was the royal councils and feudal quarrels that were comparatively remote. The Holy Land was much nearer to a plain man's house than Westminster, and immeasurably nearer than Runymede. To give a list of English kings and parliaments, without pausing for a moment upon this prodigious presence of a religious transfiguration in common life, is something the folly of which can but faintly be conveyed by a more modern parallel, with secularity and religion reversed. It is as if some Clericalist or Royalist writer should give a list of the Archbishops of Paris from 1750 to 1850, noting how one died of small-pox, another of old age, another by a curious accident of decapitation, and throughout all his record should never once mention the nature, or even the name, of the French Revolution.

7. THE PROBLEM OF THE PLANTAGENETS

It is a point of prestige with what is called the Higher Criticism in all branches to proclaim that certain popular texts and authorities are "late," and therefore apparently worthless. Two similar events are always the same event, and the later alone is even credible. This fanaticism is often in mere fact mistaken; it ignores the most common coincidences of human life: and some future critic will probably say that the tale of the Tower of Babel cannot be older than the Eiffel Tower, because there was certainly a confusion of tongues at the Paris Exhibition. Most of the mediæval remains familiar to the modern reader are necessarily "late," such as Chaucer or the Robin Hood ballads; but they are none the less, to a wiser criticism, worthy of attention and even trust. That which lingers after an epoch is generally that which lived most luxuriantly in it. It is an excellent habit to read history backwards. It is far wiser for a modern man to read the Middle Ages backwards from Shakespeare, whom he can judge for himself, and who yet is crammed with the Middle Ages, than to attempt to read them forwards from Cædmon, of whom he can know nothing, and of whom even the authorities he must trust know very little. If this be true of Shakespeare, it is even truer, of course, of Chaucer. If we really want to know what was strongest in the twelfth century, it is no bad way to ask what remained of it in the fourteenth. When the average reader turns to the "Canterbury Tales," which are still as amusing as Dickens yet as mediæval as Durham Cathedral, what is the very first question to be asked? Why, for instance, are they called Canterbury Tales; and what were the pilgrims doing on the road to Canterbury? They were, of course, taking part in a popular festival like a modern public holiday, though much more genial and leisurely. Nor are we, perhaps, prepared to accept it as a self-evident step in progress that their holidays were derived from saints, while ours are dictated by bankers.

It is almost necessary to say nowadays that a saint means a very good man. The notion of an eminence merely moral, consistent with complete stupidity or unsuccess, is a revolutionary image grown unfamiliar by its very familiarity, and needing, as do so many things of this older society, some almost preposterous modern parallel to give its original freshness and point. If we entered a foreign town and found a pillar like the Nelson Column, we should be surprised to learn that the hero on the top of it had been famous for his politeness and hilarity during a chronic toothache. If a procession came down the street with a brass band and a hero on a white horse, we should think it odd to be told that he had been very patient with a half-witted maiden aunt. Yet some such pantomime impossibility is the only measure of the innovation of the Christian idea of a popular and recognized saint. It must especially be realized that while this kind of glory was the highest, it was also in a sense the lowest. The materials of it were almost the same as those of labour and domesticity: it did not need the sword or sceptre, but rather the staff or spade. It was the ambition of poverty. All this must be approximately visualized before we catch a glimpse of the great effects of the story which lay behind the Canterbury Pilgrimage.

The first few lines of Chaucer's poem, to say nothing of thousands in the course of it, make it instantly plain that it was no case of secular revels still linked by a slight ritual to the name of some forgotten god, as may have happened in the pagan decline. Chaucer and his friends did think about St. Thomas, at least more frequently than a clerk at Margate thinks about St. Lubbock. They did definitely believe in the bodily cures wrought for them through St. Thomas, at least as firmly as the most enlightened and progressive modern can believe in those of Mrs. Eddy. Who was St. Thomas, to whose shrine the whole of that society is thus seen in the act of moving; and why was he so important? If there be a streak of sincerity in the claim to teach social and democratic history, instead of a string of kings and battles, this is the obvious and open gate by which to approach the figure which disputed England with the first Plantagenet. A real popular history should think more of his popularity even than his policy. And unquestionably thousands of ploughmen, carpenters, cooks, and yeomen, as in the motley crowd of Chaucer, knew a great deal about St. Thomas when they had never even heard of Becket.

It would be easy to detail what followed the Conquest as the feudal tangle that it was, till a prince from Anjou repeated the unifying effort of the Conqueror. It is found equally easy to write of the Red King's hunting instead of his building, which has lasted longer, and which he probably loved much more. It is easy to catalogue the questions he disputed with Anselm—leaving out the question Anselm cared most about, and which he asked with explosive simplicity, as, "Why was God a man?" All this is as simple as saying that a king died of eating lampreys, from which, however, there is little to learn nowadays, unless it be that when a modern monarch perishes of gluttony the newspapers seldom say so. But if we want to know what really happened to England in this dim epoch, I think it can be dimly but truly traced in the story of St. Thomas of Canterbury.

Henry of Anjou, who brought fresh French blood into the monarchy, brought also a refreshment of the idea for which the French have always stood: the idea in the Roman Law of something impersonal and omnipresent. It is the thing we smile at even in a small French detective story; when Justice opens a handbag or Justice runs after a cab. Henry II. really produced this impression of being a police force in person; a contemporary priest compared his restless vigilance to the bird and the fish of scripture whose way no man knoweth. Kinghood, however, meant law and not caprice; its ideal at least was a justice cheap and obvious as daylight, an atmosphere which lingers only in popular phrases about the King's English or the King's high-way. But though it tended to be egalitarian it did not, of itself, tend to be humanitarian. In modern France, as in ancient Rome, the other name of Justice has sometimes been Terror. The Frenchman especially is always a Revolutionist—and never an Anarchist. Now this effort of kings like Henry II. to rebuild on a plan like that of the Roman Law was not only, of course, crossed and entangled by countless feudal fancies and feelings in themselves as well as others, it was also conditioned by what was the corner-stone of the whole civilization. It had to happen not only with but within the Church. For a Church was to these men rather a world they lived in than a building to which they went. Without the Church the Middle Ages would have had no law, as without the Church the Reformation would have had no Bible. Many priests expounded and embellished the Roman Law, and many priests supported Henry II. And yet there was another element in the Church, stored in its first foundations like dynamite, and destined in every age to destroy and renew the world. An idealism akin to impossibilism ran down the ages parallel to all its political compromises. Monasticism itself was the throwing off of innumerable Utopias, without posterity yet with perpetuity. It had, as was proved recurrently after corrupt epochs, a strange secret of getting poor quickly; a mushroom magnificence of destitution. This wind of revolution in the crusading time caught Francis in Assissi and stripped him of his rich garments in the street. The same wind of revolution suddenly smote Thomas Becket, King Henry's brilliant and luxurious Chancellor, and drove him on to an unearthly glory and a bloody end.

Becket was a type of those historic times in which it is really very practical to be impracticable. The quarrel which tore him from his friend's side cannot be appreciated in the light of those legal and constitutional debates which the misfortunes of the seventeenth century have made so much of in more recent history. To convict St. Thomas of illegality and clerical intrigue, when he set the law of the Church against that of the State, is about as adequate as to convict St. Francis of bad heraldry when he said he was the brother of the sun and moon. There may have been heralds stupid enough to say so even in that much more logical age, but it is no sufficient way of dealing with visions or with revolutions. St. Thomas of Canterbury was a great visionary and a great revolutionist, but so far as England was concerned his revolution failed and his vision was not fulfilled. We are therefore told in the text-books little more than that he wrangled with the King about certain regulations; the most crucial being whether "criminous clerks" should be punished by the State or the Church. And this was indeed the chief text of the dispute; but to realise it we must reiterate what is hardest for modern England to understand—the nature of the Catholic Church when it was itself a government, and the permanent sense in which it was itself a revolution.

It is always the first fact that escapes notice; and the first fact about the Church was that it created a machinery of pardon, where the State could only work with a machinery of punishment. It claimed to be a divine detective who helped the criminal to escape by a plea of guilty. It was, therefore, in the very nature of the institution, that when it did punish materially it punished more lightly. If any modern man were put back in the Becket quarrel, his sympathies would certainly be torn in two; for if the King's scheme was the more rational, the Archbishop's was the more humane. And despite the horrors that darkened religious disputes long afterwards, this character was certainly in the bulk the historic character of Church government. It is admitted, for instance, that things like eviction, or the harsh treatment of tenants, was practically unknown wherever the Church was landlord. The principle lingered into more evil days in the form by which the Church authorities handed over culprits to the secular arm to be killed, even for religious offences. In modern romances this is treated as a mere hypocrisy; but the man who treats every human inconsistency as a hypocrisy is himself a hypocrite about his own inconsistencies.

Our world, then, cannot understand St. Thomas, any more than St. Francis, without accepting very simply a flaming and even fantastic charity, by which the great Archbishop undoubtedly stands for the victims of this world, where the wheel of fortune grinds the faces of the poor. He may well have been too idealistic; he wished to protect the Church as a sort of earthly paradise, of which the rules might seem to him as paternal as those of heaven, but might well seem to the King as capricious as those of fairyland. But if the priest was too idealistic, the King was really too practical; it is intrinsically true to say he was too practical to succeed in practice. There re-enters here, and runs, I think, through all English history, the rather indescribable truth I have suggested about the Conqueror; that perhaps he was hardly impersonal enough for a pure despot. The real moral of our mediæval story is, I think, subtly contrary to Carlyle's vision of a stormy strong man to hammer and weld the state like a smith. Our strong men were too strong for us, and too strong for themselves. They were too strong for their own aim of a just and equal monarchy. The smith broke upon the anvil the sword of state that he was hammering for himself. Whether or no this will serve as a key to the very complicated story of our kings and barons, it is the exact posture of Henry II. to his rival. He became lawless out of sheer love of law. He also stood, though in a colder and more remote manner, for the whole people against feudal oppression; and if his policy had succeeded in its purity, it would at least have made impossible the privilege and capitalism of later times. But that bodily restless-ness which stamped and spurned the furniture was a symbol of him; it was some such thing that prevented him and his heirs from sitting as quietly on their throne as the heirs of St. Louis. He thrust again and again at the tough intangibility of the priests' Utopianism like a man fighting a ghost; he answered transcendental defi-ances with baser material persecutions; and at last, on a dark and, I think, decisive day in English history, his word sent four feudal murderers into the cloisters of Canterbury, who went there to destroy a traitor and who created a saint.

At the grave of the dead man broke forth what can only be called an epidemic of healing. For miracles so narrated there is the same evidence as for half the facts of history; and any one denying them must deny them upon a dogma. But something followed which would seem to modern civilization even more monstrous than a miracle. If the reader can imagine Mr. Cecil Rhodes submitting to be horsewhipped by a Boer in St. Paul's Cathedral, as an apology for some indefensible death inci-dental to the Jameson Raid, he will form but a faint idea of what was meant when Henry II. was beaten by monks at the tomb of his vassal and enemy. The modern parallel called up is comic, but the truth is that mediæval actualities have a violence that does seem comic to our conventions. The Catholics of that age were driven by two dominant thoughts: the all-importance of penitence as an answer to sin, and the all-importance of vivid and evident external acts as a proof of penitence. Extravagant humiliation after extravagant pride for them restored the balance of sanity. The point is worth stressing, because without it moderns make neither head nor tail of the period. Green gravely suggests, for instance, of Henry's ancestor Fulk of Anjou, that his tyrannies and frauds were further blackened by "low superstition," which led him to be dragged in a halter round a shrine, scourged and screaming for the mercy of God. Mediævals would simply have said that such a man might well scream for it, but his scream was the only logical comment he could make. But they would have quite refused to see why the scream should be added to the sins and not subtracted from them. They would have thought it simply muddle-headed to have the same horror at a man for being horribly sinful and for being horribly sorry.

But it may be suggested, I think, though with the doubt proper to ignorance, that the Angevin ideal of the King's justice lost more by the death of St. Thomas than was instantly apparent in the horror of Christendom, the canonization of the victim and the public penance of the tyrant. These things indeed were in a sense temporary; the King recovered the power to judge clerics, and many later kings and justiciars continued the monarchical plan. But I would suggest, as a possible clue to puzzling after events, that here and by this murderous stroke the crown lost what should have been the silent and massive support of its whole policy. I mean that it lost the people.

It need not be repeated that the case for despotism is democratic. As a rule its cruelty to the strong is kindness to the weak. An autocrat cannot be judged as a historical character by his relations with other historical characters. His true applause comes not from the few actors on the lighted stage of aristocracy, but from that enormous audience which must always sit in darkness throughout the drama. The king who helps numberless helps nameless men, and when he flings his widest largesse he is a Christian doing good by stealth. This sort of monarchy was certainly a mediæval ideal, nor need it necessarily fail as a reality. French kings were never so merciful to the people as when they were merciless to the peers; and it is probably true that a Czar who was a great lord to his intimates was often a little father in innumerable little homes. It is overwhelmingly probable that such a central power, though it might at last have deserved destruction in England as in France, would in England as in France have prevented the few from seizing and holding all the wealth and power to this day. But in England it broke off short, through something of which the slaying of St. Thomas may well have been the supreme example. It was something overstrained and startling and against the instincts of the people. And of what was meant in the Middle Ages by that very powerful and rather peculiar thing, the people, I shall speak in the next chapter.

In any case this conjecture finds support in the ensuing events. It is not merely that, just as the great but personal plan of the Conqueror collapsed after all into the chaos of the Stephen transition, so the great but personal plan of the first Plantagenet collapsed into the chaos of the Barons' Wars. When all allowance is made for constitutional fictions and afterthoughts, it does seem likely that here for the first time some moral strength deserted the monarchy. The character of Henry's second son John (for Richard belongs rather to the last chapter) stamped it with something accidental and yet symbolic. It was not that John was a mere black blot on the pure gold of the Plantagenets, the texture was much more mixed and continuous; but he really was a discredited Plantagenet, and as it were a damaged Plantagenet. It was not that he was much more of a bad man than many opposed to him, but he was the kind of bad man whom bad men and good do combine to oppose. In a sense subtler than that of the legal and parliamentary logic-chopping invented long afterwards, he certainly managed to put the Crown in the wrong. Nobody suggested that the barons of Stephen's time starved men in dungeons to promote political liberty, or hung them up by the heels as a symbolic request for a free parliament. In the reign of John and his son it was still the barons, and not in the least the people, who seized the power; but there did begin to appear a *case* for their seizing it, for contemporaries as well as constitutional historians afterwards. John, in one of his diplomatic doublings, had put England into the papal care, as an estate is put in Chancery. And unluckily the Pope, whose counsels had generally been mild and liberal, was then in his death-grapple with the Germanic Emperor and wanted every penny he could get to win. His winning was a blessing to Europe, but a curse to England, for he used the island as a mere treasury for this foreign war. In this and other matters the baronial party began to have something like a principle, which is the backbone of a policy. Much conventional history that connects their councils with a thing like our House of Commons is as far-fetched as it would be to say that the Speaker wields a Mace like those which the barons brandished in battle. Simon de Montfort was not an enthusiast for the Whig theory of the British Constitution, but he was an enthusiast for something. He founded a parliament in a fit of considerable absence of mind; but it was with true presence of mind, in the responsible and even religious sense which had made his father so savage a Crusader against heretics, that he laid about him with his great sword before he fell at Evesham.

Magna Carta was not a step towards democracy, but it was a step away from despotism. If we hold that double truth firmly, we have something like a key to the rest of English history. A rather loose aristocracy not only gained but often deserved the name of liberty. And the history of the English can be most briefly summarized by taking the French motto of "Liberty, Equality, and Fraternity," and noting that the English have sincerely loved the first and lost the other two.

In the contemporary complication much could be urged both for the Crown and the new and more national rally of the nobility. But it was a complication, whereas a miracle is a plain matter that any man can understand. The possibilities or impossibilities of St. Thomas Becket were left a riddle for history; the white flame of his audacious theocracy was frustrated, and his work cut short like a fairy tale left untold. But his memory passed into the care of the common people, and with them he was more active dead than alive—yes, even more busy. In the next chapter we shall consider what was meant in the Middle Ages by the common people, and how uncommon we should think it to-day. And in the last chapter we have already seen how in the Crusading age the strangest things grew homely, and men fed on travellers' tales when there were no national newspapers. A many-coloured pageant of martyrology on numberless walls and windows had familiarized the most ignorant with alien cruelties in many climes; with a bishop flayed by Danes or a virgin burned by Saracens, with one saint stoned by Jews and another hewn in pieces by negroes. I cannot think it was a small matter that among these images one of the most magnificent had met his death but lately at the hands of an English monarch. There was at least something akin to the primitive and epical romances of that period in the tale of those two mighty friends, one of whom struck too hard and slew the other. It may even have been so early as this that something was judged in silence; and for the multitude rested on the Crown a mysterious seal of insecurity like that of Cain, and of exile on the English kings.

8. THE MEANING OF MERRY ENGLAND

The mental trick by which the first half of English history has been wholly dwarfed and dehumanized is a very simple one. It consists in telling only the story of the professional destroyers and then complaining that the whole story is one of destruction. A king is at the best a sort of crowned executioner; all government is an ugly necessity; and if it was then uglier it was for the most part merely because it was more difficult. What we call the Judges' circuits were first rather the King's raids. For a time the criminal class was so strong that ordinary civil government was conducted by a sort of civil war. When the social enemy was caught at all he was killed or savagely maimed. The King could not take Pentonville Prison about with him on wheels. I am far from denying that there was a real element of cruelty in the Middle Ages; but the point here is that it was concerned with one side of life, which is cruel at the best; and that this involved more cruelty for the same reason that it involved more courage. When we think of our ancestors as the men who inflicted tortures, we ought sometimes to think of them as the men who defied them. But the modern critic of mediævalism commonly looks only at these crooked shadows and not at the common daylight of the Middle Ages. When he has got over his indignant astonishment at the fact that fighters fought and that hangmen hanged, he assumes that any other ideas there may have been were ineffectual and fruitless. He despises the monk for avoiding the very same activities which he despises the warrior for cultivating. And he insists that the arts of war were sterile, without even admitting the possibility that the arts of peace were productive. But the truth is that it is precisely in the arts of peace, and in the type of production, that the Middle Ages stand singular and unique. This is not eulogy but history; an informed man must recognize this productive peculiarity even if he happens to hate it. The melodramatic things currently called mediæval are much older and more universal; such as the sport of tournament or the use of torture. The tournament was indeed a Christian and liberal advance on the gladiatorial show, since the lords risked themselves and not merely their slaves. Torture, so far from being peculiarly mediæval, was copied from pagan Rome and its most rationalist political science; and its application to others besides slaves was really part of the slow mediæval extinction of slavery. Torture, indeed, is a logical thing common in states innocent of fanaticism, as in the great agnostic empire of China. What was really arresting and remarkable about the Middle Ages, as the Spartan discipline was peculiar to Sparta, or the Russian communes typical of Russia, was precisely its positive social scheme of production, of the making, building and growing of all the good things of life.

For the tale told in a book like this cannot really touch on mediæval England at all. The dynasties and the parliaments passed like a changing cloud and across a stable and fruitful landscape. The institutions which affected the masses can be compared to corn or fruit trees in one practical sense at least, that they grew upwards from below. There may have been better societies, and assuredly we have not to look far for worse; but it is doubtful if there was ever so spontaneous a society. We cannot do justice, for instance, to the local government of that epoch, even where it was very faulty and fragmentary, by any comparisons with the plans of local government laid down to-day. Modern local government always comes from above; it is at best granted; it is more often merely imposed. The modern English oligarchy, the modern German Empire, are necessarily more efficient in making municipalities upon a plan, or rather a pattern. The mediævals not only had self-government, but their self-government was self-made. They did indeed, as the central powers of the national monarchies grew stronger, seek and procure the stamp of state approval; but it was approval of a popular fact already in existence. Men banded together in guilds and parishes long before Local Government Acts were dreamed of. Like charity, which was worked in the same way, their Home Rule began at home. The reactions of recent centuries have left most educated men bankrupt of the corporate imagination required even to imagine this. They only think of a mob as a thing that breaks things —even if they admit it is right to break them. But the mob made these things. An artist mocked as many-headed, an artist with many eyes and hands, created these masterpieces. And if the modern sceptic, in his detestation of the democratic ideal, complains of my calling them masterpieces, a simple answer will for the moment serve. It is enough to reply that the very word "masterpiece" is borrowed from the terminology of the mediæval craftsmen. But such points in the Guild System can be considered a little later; here we are only concerned with the quite spontaneous springing upwards of all these social institutions, such as they were. They rose in the streets like a silent rebellion; like a still and statuesque riot. In modern constitutional countries there are practically no political institutions thus given by the people; all are received by the people. There is only one thing that stands in our midst, attenuated and threatened, but enthroned in some power like a ghost of the Middle Ages: the Trades Unions.

In agriculture, what had happened to the land was like a universal landslide. But by a prodigy beyond the catastrophes of geology it may be said that the land had slid uphill. Rural civilization was on a wholly new and much higher level; yet there was no great social convulsions or apparently even great social campaigns to explain it. It is possibly a solitary instance in history of men thus falling upwards; at least of outcasts falling on their feet or vagrants straying into the promised land. Such a thing could not be and was not a mere accident; yet, if we go by conscious political plans, it was something like a miracle. There had appeared, like a subterranean race cast up to the sun, something unknown to the august civilization of the Roman Empire—a peasantry. At the beginning of the Dark Ages the great pagan cosmopolitan society now grown Christian was as much a slave state as old South Carolina. By the fourteenth century it was almost as much a state of peasant proprietors as modern France. No laws had been passed against slavery; no dogmas even had condemned it by definition; no war had been waged against it, no new race or ruling caste had repudiated it; but it was gone. This startling and silent transformation is perhaps the best measure of the pressure of popular life in the Middle Ages, of how fast it was making new things in its spiritual factory. Like everything else in the mediæval revolution, from its cathedrals to its ballads, it was as anonymous as it was enormous. It is admitted that the conscious and active emancipators everywhere were the parish priests and the religious brotherhoods; but no name among them has survived and no man of them has reaped his reward in this world. Countless Clarksons and innumerable Wilberforces, without political machinery or public fame, worked at deathbeds and confessionals in all the villages of Europe; and the vast system of slavery vanished. It was probably the widest work ever done which was voluntary on both sides; and the Middle Ages was in this and other things the age of volunteers. It is possible enough to state roughly the stages through which the thing passed; but such a statement does not explain the loosening of the grip of the great slave-owners; and it cannot be explained except psychologically. The Catholic type of Christianity was not merely an element, it was a climate; and in that climate the slave would not grow. I have already suggested, touching that transformation of the Roman Empire which was the background of all these centuries, how a mystical view of man's dignity must have this effect. A table that walked and talked, or a stool that flew with wings out of window, would be about as workable a thing as an immortal chattel. But though here as everywhere the spirit explains the processes, and the processes cannot even plausibly explain the spirit, these processes involve two very practical points, without which we cannot understand how this great popular civilization was created—or how it was destroyed.

What we call the manors were originally the *villae* of the pagan lords, each with its population of slaves. Under this process, however it be explained, what had occurred was the diminishment of the lords' claim to the whole profit of a slave estate, by which it became a claim to the profit of part of it, and dwindled at last to certain dues or customary payments to the lord, having paid which the slave could enjoy not only the use of the land but the profit of it. It must be remembered that over a great part, and especially very important parts, of the whole territory, the lords were abbots, magistrates elected by a mystical communism and themselves often of peasant birth. Men not only obtained a fair amount of justice under their care, but a fair amount of freedom even from their carelessness. But two details of the development are very vital. First, as has been hinted elsewhere, the slave was long in the intermediate status of a serf. This meant that while the land was entitled to the services of the man, he was equally entitled to the support of the land. He could not be evicted; he could not even, in the modern fashion, have his rent raised. At the beginning it was merely that the slave was owned, but at least he could not be disowned. At the end he had really become a small landlord, merely because it was not the lord that owned him, but the land. It is hardly unsafe to suggest that in this (by one of the paradoxes of this extraordinary period) the very fixity of serfdom was a service to freedom. The new peasant inherited something of the stability of the slave. He did not come to life in a competitive scramble where everybody was trying to snatch his freedom from him. He found himself among neighbours who already regarded his presence as normal and his frontiers as natural frontiers, and among whom all-powerful customs crushed all experiments in competition. By a trick or overturn no romancer has dared to put in a tale, this prisoner had become the governor of his own prison. For a little time it was almost true that an Englishman's house was his castle, because it had been built strong enough to be his dungeon.

The other notable element was this: that when the produce of the land began by custom to be cut up and only partially transmitted to the lord, the remainder was generally subdivided into two types of property. One the serfs enjoyed severally, in private patches, while the other they enjoyed in common, and generally in common with the lord. Thus arose the momentously important mediæval institutions of the Common Land, owned side by side with private land. It was an alternative and a refuge. The mediævals, except when they were monks, were none of them Communists; but they were all, as it were, potential Communists. It is typical of the dark and dehumanized picture now drawn of the period that our romances constantly describe a broken man as falling back on the forests and the outlaw's den, but never describe him as falling back on the common land, which was a much more common incident. Mediævalism believed in mending its broken men; and as the idea existed in the communal life for monks, it existed in the communal land for peasants. It was their great green hospital, their free and airy workhouse. A Common was not a naked and negative thing like the scrub or heath we call a Common on the edges of the suburbs. It was a reserve of wealth like a reserve of grain in a barn; it was deliberately kept back as a balance, as we talk of a balance at the bank. Now these provisions for a healthier distribution of property would by themselves show any man of imagination that a real moral effort had been made towards social justice; that it could not have been mere evolutionary accident that slowly turned the slave into a serf, and the serf into a peasant proprietor. But if anybody still thinks that mere blind luck, without any groping for the light, had somehow brought about the peasant condition in place of the agrarian slave estate, he has only to turn to what was happening in all the other callings and affairs of humanity. Then he will cease to doubt. For he will find the same mediæval men busy upon a social scheme which points as plainly in effect to pity and a craving for equality. And it is a system which could no more be produced by accident than one of their cathedrals could be built by an earthquake.

Most work beyond the primary work of agriculture was guarded by the egalitarian vigilance of the Guilds. It is hard to find any term to measure the distance between this system and modern society; one can only approach it first by the faint traces it has left. Our daily life is littered with a debris of the Middle Ages, especially of dead words which no longer carry their meaning. I have already suggested one example. We hardly call up the picture of a return to Christian Communism whenever we mention Wimbledon Common. This truth descends to such trifles as the titles which we write on letters and postcards. The puzzling and truncated monosyllable "Esq." is a pathetic relic of a remote evolution from chivalry to snobbery. No two historic things could well be more different than an esquire and a squire. The first was above all things an incomplete and probationary position—the tadpole of knighthood; the second is above all things a complete and assured position—the status of the owners and rulers of rural England throughout recent centuries. Our esquires did not win their estates till they had given up any particular fancy for winning their spurs. Esquire does not mean squire, and esq. does not mean anything. But it remains on our letters a little wriggle in pen and ink and an indecipherable hieroglyph twisted by the strange turns of our history, which have turned a military discipline into a pacific oligarchy, and that into a mere plutocracy at last. And there are similar historic riddles to be unpicked in the similar forms of social address. There is something singularly forlorn about the modern word "Mister." Even in sound it has a simpering feebleness which marks the shrivelling of the strong word from which it came. Nor, indeed, is the symbol of the mere sound inaccurate. I remember seeing a German story of Samson in which he bore the unassuming name of Simson, which surely shows Samson very much shorn. There is something of the same dismal *diminuendo* in the evolution of a Master into a Mister.

The very vital importance of the word "Master" is this. A Guild was, very broadly speaking, a Trade Union in which every man was his own employer. That is, a man could not work at any trade unless he would join the league and accept the laws of that trade; but he worked in his own shop with his own tools, and the whole profit went to himself. But the word "employer" marks a modern deficiency which makes the modern use of the word "master" quite inexact. A master meant something quite other and greater than a "boss." It meant a master of the work, where it now means only a master of the workmen. It is an elementary character of Capitalism that a shipowner need not know the right end of a ship, or a landowner have even seen the landscape, that the owner of a goldmine may be interested in nothing but old pewter, or the owner of a railway travel exclusively in balloons. He may be a more successful capitalist if he has a hobby of his own business; he is often a more successful capitalist if he has the sense to leave it to a manager; but economically he can control the business because he is a capitalist, not because he has any kind of hobby or any kind of sense. The highest grade in the Guild system was a Master, and it meant a mastery of the business. To take the term created by the colleges in the same epoch, all the mediæval bosses were Masters of Arts. The other grades were the journeyman and the apprentice; but like the corresponding degrees at the universities, they were grades through which every common man could pass. They were not social classes; they were degrees and not castes. This is the whole point of the recurrent romance about the apprentice marrying his master's daughter. The master would not be surprised at such a thing, any more than an M.A. would swell with aristocratic indignation when his daughter married a B.A.

When we pass from the strictly educational hierarchy to the strictly egalitarian ideal, we find again that the remains of the thing to-day are so distorted and disconnected as to be comic. There are City Companies which inherit the coats of arms and the immense relative wealth of the old Guilds, and inherit nothing else. Even what is good about them is not what was good about the Guilds. In one case we shall find something like a Worshipful Company of Bricklayers, in which, it is unnecessary to say, there is not a single bricklayer or anybody who has ever known a bricklayer, but in which the senior partners of a few big businesses in the City, with a few faded military men with a taste in cookery, tell each other in after-dinner speeches that it has been the glory of their lives to make allegorical bricks without straw. In another case we shall find a Worshipful Company of Whitewashers who do deserve their name, in the sense that many of them employ a large number of other people to whitewash. These Companies support large charities and often doubtless very valuable charities; but their object is quite different from that of the old charities of the Guilds. The aim of the Guild charities was the same as the aim of the Common Land. It was to resist inequality—or, as some earnest old gentlemen of the last generation would probably put it, to resist evolution. It was to ensure, not only that bricklaying should survive and succeed, but that every bricklayer should survive and succeed. It sought to rebuild the ruins of any bricklayer, and to give any faded whitewasher a new white coat. It was the whole aim of the Guilds to cobble their cobblers like their shoes and clout their clothiers with their clothes; to strengthen the weakest link, or go after the hundredth sheep; in short, to keep the row of little shops unbroken like a line of battle. It resisted the growth of a big shop like the growth of a dragon. Now even the whitewashers of the Whitewashers Company will not pretend that it exists to prevent a small shop being swallowed by a big shop, or that it has done anything whatever to prevent it. At the best the kindness it would show to a bankrupt whitewasher would be a kind of compensation; it would not be reinstatement; it would not be the restoration of status in an industrial system. So careful of the type it seems, so careless of the single life; and by that very modern evolutionary philosophy the type itself has been destroyed. The old Guilds, with the same object of equality, of course, insisted peremptorily upon the same level system of payment and treatment which is a point of complaint against the modern Trades Unions. But they insisted also, as the Trades Unions cannot do, upon a high standard of craftsmanship, which still astonishes the world in the corners of perishing buildings or the colours of broken glass. There is no artist or art critic who will not concede, however distant his own style from the Gothic school, that there was in this time a nameless but universal artistic touch in the moulding of the very tools of life. Accident has preserved the rudest sticks and stools and pots and pans which have suggestive shapes as if they were possessed not by devils but by elves. For they were, indeed, as compared with subsequent systems, produced in the incredible fairyland of a free country.

That the most mediæval of modern institutions, the Trades Unions, do not fight for the same ideal of æsthetic finish is true and certainly tragic; but to make it a matter of blame is wholly to misunderstand the tragedy. The Trades Unions are confederations of men without property, seeking to balance its absence by numbers and the necessary character of their labour. The Guilds were confederations of men with property, seeking to ensure each man in the possession of that property. This is, of course, the only condition of affairs in which property can properly be said to exist at all. We should not speak of a negro community in which most men were white, but the rare negroes were giants. We should not conceive a married community in which most men were bachelors, and three men had harems. A married community means a community where most people are married; not a community where one or two people are very much married. A propertied community means a community where most people have property; not a community where there are a few capitalists. But in fact the Guildsmen (as also, for that matter, the serfs, semi-serfs and peasants) were much richer than can be realized even from the fact that the Guilds protected the possession of houses, tools, and just payment. The surplus is self-evident upon any just study of the prices of the period, when all deductions have been made, of course, for the different value of the actual coinage. When a man could get a goose or a gallon of ale for one or two of the smallest and commonest coins, the matter is in no way affected by the name of those coins. Even where the individual wealth was severely limited, the collective wealth was very large—the wealth of the Guilds, of the parishes, and especially of the monastic estates. It is important to remember this fact in the subsequent history of England.

The next fact to note is that the local government grew out of things like the Guild system, and not the system from the government. In sketching the sound principles of this lost society, I shall not, of course, be supposed by any sane person to be describing a moral paradise, or to be implying that it was free from the faults and fights and sorrows that harass human life in all times, and certainly not least in our own time. There was a fair amount of rioting and fighting in connection with the Guilds; and there was especially for some time a combative rivalry between the guilds of merchants who sold things and those of craftsmen who made them, a conflict in which the craftsmen on the whole prevailed. But whichever party may have been predominant, it was the heads of the Guild who became the heads of the town, and not vice versa. The stiff survivals of this once very spontaneous uprising can again be seen in the now anomalous constitution of the Lord Mayor and the Livery of the City of London. We are told so monotonously that the government of our fathers reposed upon arms, that it is valid to insist that this, their most intimate and everyday sort of government, was wholly based upon tools; a government in which the workman's tool became the sceptre. Blake, in one of his symbolic fantasies, suggests that in the Golden Age the gold and gems should be taken from the hilt of the sword and put upon the handle of the plough. But something very like this did happen in the interlude of this mediæval democracy, fermenting under the crust of mediæval monarchy and aristocracy; where productive implements often took on the pomp of heraldry. The Guilds often exhibited emblems and pageantry so compact of their most prosaic uses, that we can only parallel them by imagining armorial tabards, or even religious vestments, woven out of a navy's corduroys or a coster's pearl buttons.

Two more points must be briefly added; and the rough sketch of this now foreign and even fantastic state will be as complete as it can be made here. Both refer to the links between this popular life and the politics which are conventially the whole of history. The first, and for that age the most evident, is the Charter. To recur once more to the parallel of Trades Unions, as convenient for the casual reader of to-day, the Charter of a Guild roughly corresponded to that "recognition" for which the railwaymen and other trades unionists asked some years ago, without success. By this they had the authority of the King, the central or national government; and this was of great moral weight with mediævals, who always conceived of freedom as a positive status, not as a negative escape: they had none of the modern romanticism which makes liberty akin to loneliness. Their view remains in the phrase about giving a man the freedom of a city: they had no desire to give him the freedom of a wilderness. To say that they had also the authority of the Church is something of an understatement; for religion ran like a rich thread through the rude tapestry of these popular things while they were still merely popular; and many a trade society must have had a patron saint long before it had a royal seal. The other point is that it was from these municipal groups already in existence that the first men were chosen for the largest and perhaps the last of the great mediæval experiments: the Parliament.

We have all read at school that Simon de Montfort and Edward I., when they first summoned Commons to council, chiefly as advisers on local taxation, called "two burgesses" from every town. If we had read a little more closely, those simple words would have given away the whole secret of the lost mediæval civilization. We had only to ask what burgesses were, and whether they grew on trees. We should immediately have discovered that England was full of little parliaments, out of which the great parliament was made. And if it be a matter of wonder that the great council (still called in quaint archaism by its old title of the House of Commons) is the only one of these popular or elective corporations of which we hear much in our books of history, the explanation, I fear, is simple and a little sad. It is that the Parliament was the one among these mediæval creations which ultimately consented to betray and to destroy the rest.

9. NATIONALITY AND THE FRENCH WARS

If any one wishes to know what we mean when we say that Christendom was and is one culture, or one civilization, there is a rough but plain way of putting it. It is by asking what is the most common, or rather the most commonplace, of all the uses of the word "Christian." There is, of course, the highest use of all; but it has nowadays many other uses. Sometimes a Christian means an Evangelical. Sometimes, and more recently, a Christian means a Quaker. Sometimes a Christian means a modest person who believes that he bears a resemblance to Christ. But it has long had one meaning in casual speech among common people, and it means a culture or a civilization. Ben Gunn on Treasure Island did not actually say to Jim Hawkins, "I feel myself out of touch with a certain type of civilization"; but he did say, "I haven't tasted Christian food." The old wives in a village looking at a lady with short hair and trousers do not indeed say, "We perceive a divergence between her culture and our own"; but they do say, "Why can't she dress like a Christian?" That the sentiment has thus soaked down to the simplest and even stupidest daily talk is but one evidence that Christendom was a very real thing. But it was also, as we have seen, a very localized thing, especially in the Middle Ages. And that very lively localism the Christian faith and affections encouraged led at last to an excessive and exclusive parochialism. There were rival shrines of the same saint, and a sort of duel between two statues of the same divinity. By a process it is now our difficult duty to follow, a real estrangement between European peoples began. Men began to feel that foreigners did not eat or drink like Christians, and even, when the philosophic schism came, to doubt if they were Christians.

There was, indeed, much more than this involved. While the internal structure of mediævalism was thus parochial and largely popular, in the greater affairs, and especially the external affairs, such as peace and war, most (though by no means all) of what was mediæval was monarchical. To see what the kings came to mean we must glance back at the great background, as of darkness and daybreak, against which the first figures of our history have already appeared. That background was the war with the barbarians. While it lasted Christendom was not only one nation but more like one city—and a besieged city. Wessex was but one wall or Paris one tower of it; and in one tongue and spirit Bede might have chronicled the siege of Paris or Abbo sung the song of Alfred. What followed was a conquest and a conversion; all the end of the Dark Ages and the dawn of mediævalism is full of the evangelizing of barbarism. And it is the paradox of the Crusades that though the Saracen was superficially more civilized than the Christian, it was a sound instinct which saw him also to be in spirit a destroyer. In the simpler case of northern heathenry the civilization spread with a simpler progress. But it was not till the end of the Middle Ages, and close on the Reformation, that the people of Prussia, the wild land lying beyond Germany, were baptized at all. A flippant person, if he permitted himself a profane confusion with vaccination, might almost be inclined to suggest that for some reason it didn't "take" even then.

The barbarian peril was thus brought under bit by bit, and even in the case of Islam the alien power which could not be crushed was evidently curbed. The Crusades became hopeless, but they also became needless. As these fears faded the princes of Europe, who had come together to face them, were left facing each other. They had more leisure to find that their own captaincies clashed; but this would easily have been overruled, or would have produced a petty riot, had not the true creative spontaneity, of which we have spoken in the local life, tended to real variety. Royalties found they were representatives almost without knowing it; and many a king insisting on a genealogical tree or a title-deed found he spoke for the forests and the songs of a whole country-side. In England especially the transition is typified in the accident which raised to the throne one of the noblest men of the Middle Ages.

Edward I. came clad in all the splendours of his epoch. He had taken the Cross and fought the Saracens; he had been the only worthy foe of Simon de Montfort in those baronial wars which, as we have seen, were the first sign (however faint) of a serious theory that England should be ruled by its barons rather than its kings. He proceeded, like Simon de Montfort, and more solidly, to develop the great mediæval institution of a parliament. As has been said, it was superimposed on the existing parish democracies, and was first merely the summoning of local representatives to advise on local taxation. Indeed its rise was one with the rise of what we now call taxation; and there is thus a thread of theory leading to its latter claims to have the sole right of taxing. But in the beginning it was an instrument of the most equitable kings, and notably an instrument of Edward I. He often quarrelled with his parliaments and may sometimes have displeased his people (which has never been at all the same thing), but on the whole he was supremely the representative sovereign. In this connection one curious and difficult question may be considered here, though it marks the end of a story that began with the Norman Conquest. It is pretty certain that he was never more truly a representative king, one might say a republican king, than in the fact that he expelled the Jews. The problem is so much misunderstood and mixed with notions of a stupid spite against a gifted and historic race as such, that we must pause for a paragraph upon it.

The Jews in the Middle Ages were as powerful as they were unpopular. They were the capitalists of the age, the men with wealth banked ready for use. It is very tenable that in this way they were useful; it is certain that in this way they were used. It is also quite fair to say that in this way they were ill-used. The ill-usage was not indeed that suggested at random in romances, which mostly revolve on the one idea that their teeth were pulled out. Those who know this as a story about King John generally do not know the rather important fact that it was a story against King John. It is probably doubtful; it was only insisted on as exceptional; and it was, by that very insistence, obviously regarded as disreputable. But the real unfairness of the Jews' position was deeper and more distressing to a sensitive and highly civilized people. They might reasonably say that Christian kings and nobles, and even Christian popes and bishops, used for Christian purposes (such as the Crusades and the cathedrals) the money that could only be accumulated in such mountains by a usury they inconsistently denounced as unchristian; and then, when worse times came, gave up the Jew to the fury of the poor, whom that useful usury had ruined. That was the real case for the Jew; and no doubt he really felt himself oppressed. Unfortunately it was the case for the Christians that they, with at least equal reason, felt him as the oppressor; and that *mutual* charge of tyranny is the Semitic trouble in all times. It is certain that in popular sentiment, this Anti-Semitism was not excused as uncharitableness, but simply regarded as charity. Chaucer puts his curse on Hebrew cruelty into the mouth of the soft-hearted prioress, who wept when she saw a mouse in a trap; and it was when Edward, breaking the rule by which the rulers had hitherto fostered their bankers' wealth, flung the alien financiers out of the land, that his people probably saw him most plainly at once as a knight errant and a tender father of his people.

Whatever the merits of this question, such a portrait of Edward was far from false. He was the most just and conscientious type of mediæval monarch; and it is exactly this fact that brings into relief the new force which was to cross his path and in strife with which he died. While he was just, he was also eminently legal. And it must be remembered, if we would not merely read back ourselves into the past, that much of the dispute of the time was legal; the adjustment of dynastic and feudal differences not yet felt to be anything else. In this spirit Edward was asked to arbitrate by the rival claimants to the Scottish crown; and in this sense he seems to have arbitrated quite honestly. But his legal, or, as some would say, pedantic mind made the proviso that the Scottish king as such was already under his suzerainty, and he probably never understood the spirit he called up against him; for that spirit had as yet no name. We call it to-day Nationalism. Scotland resisted; and the adventures of an outlawed knight named Wallace soon furnished it with one of those legends which are more important than history. In a way that was then at least equally practical, the Catholic priests of Scotland became especially the patriotic and Anti-English party; as indeed they remained even throughout the Reformation. Wallace was defeated and executed; but the heather was already on fire; and the espousal of the new national cause by one of Edward's own knights named Bruce, seemed to the old king a mere betrayal of feudal equity. He died in a final fury at the head of a new invasion upon the very border of Scotland. With his last words the great king commanded that his bones should be borne in front of the battle; and the bones, which were of gigantic size, were eventually buried with the epitaph, "Here lies Edward the Tall, who was the hammer of the Scots." It was a true epitaph, but in a sense exactly opposite to its intention. He was their hammer, but he did not break but make them; for he smote them on an anvil and he forged them into a sword.

That coincidence or course of events, which must often be remarked in this story, by which (for whatever reason) our most powerful kings did not somehow leave their power secure, showed itself in the next reign, when the baronial quarrels were resumed and the northern kingdom, under Bruce, cut itself finally free by the stroke of Bannockburn. Otherwise the reign is a mere interlude, and it is with the succeeding one that we find the new national tendency yet further developed. The great French wars, in which England won so much glory, were opened by Edward III., and grew more and more nationalist. But even to feel the transition of the time we must first realize that the third Edward made as strictly legal and dynastic a claim to France as the first Edward had made to Scotland; the claim was far weaker in substance, but it was equally conventional in form. He thought, or said, he had a claim on a kingdom as a squire might say he had a claim on an estate; superficially it was an affair for the English and French lawyers. To read into this that the people were sheep bought and sold is to misunderstand all mediæval history; sheep have no trade union. The English arms owed much of their force to the class of the free yeomen; and the success of the infantry, especially of the archery, largely stood for that popular element which had already unhorsed the high French chivalry at Courtrai. But the point is this; that while the lawyers were talking about the Salic Law, the soldiers, who would once have been talking about guild law or glebe law, were already talking about English law and French law. The French were first in this tendency to see something outside the township, the trade brotherhood, the feudal dues, or the village common. The whole history of the change can be seen in the fact that the French had early begun to call the nation the Greater Land. France was the first of nations and has remained the norm of nations, the only one which is a nation and nothing else. But in the collision the English grew equally corporate; and a true patriotic applause probably hailed the victories of Crecy and Poitiers, as it certainly hailed the later victory of Agincourt. The latter did not indeed occur until after an interval of internal revolutions in England, which will be considered on a later page; but as regards the growth of nationalism, the French wars were continuous. And the English tradition that followed after Agincourt was continuous also. It is embodied in rude and spirited ballads before the great Elizabethans. The Henry V. of Shakespeare is not indeed the Henry V. of history; yet he is more historic. He is not only a saner and more genial but a more important person. For the tradition of the whole adventure was not that of Henry, but of the populace who turned Henry into Harry. There were a thousand Harries in the army at Agincourt, and not one. For the figure that Shakespeare framed out of the legends of the great victory is largely the figure that all men saw as the Englishman of the Middle Ages. He did not really talk in poetry, like Shakespeare's hero, but he would have liked to. Not being able to do so, he sang; and the English people principally appear in contemporary impressions as the singing people. They were evidently not only expansive but exaggerative; and perhaps it was not only in battle that they drew the long bow. That fine farcical imagery, which has descended to the comic songs and common speech of the English poor even to-day, had its happy infancy when England thus became a nation; though the modern poor, under the pressure of economic progress, have partly lost the gaiety and kept only the humour. But in that early April of patriotism the new unity of the State still sat lightly upon them; and a cobbler in Henry's army, who would at home have thought first that it was the day of St. Crispin of the Cobblers, might truly as well as sincerely have hailed the splintering of the French lances in a storm of arrows, and cried, "St. George for Merry England."

Human things are uncomfortably complex, and while it was the April of patriotism it was the Autumn of mediæval society. In the next chapter I shall try to trace the forces that were disintegrating the civilization; and even here, after the first victories, it is necessary to insist on the bitterness and barren ambition that showed itself more and more in the later stages, as the long French wars dragged on. France was at the time far less happy than England—wasted by the treason of its nobles and the weakness of its kings almost as much as by the invasion of the islanders. And yet it was this very despair and humiliation that seemed at last to rend the sky, and let in the light of what it is hard for the coldest historian to call anything but a miracle.

It may be this apparent miracle that has apparently made Nationalism eternal. It may be conjectured, though the question is too difficult to be developed here, that there was something in the great moral change which turned the Roman Empire into Christendom, by which each great thing, to which it afterwards gave birth, was baptized into a promise, or at least into a hope of permanence. It may be that each of its ideas was, as it were, mixed with immortality. Certainly something of this kind can be seen in the conception which turned marriage from a contract into a sacrament. But whatever the cause, it is certain that even for the most secular types of our own time their relation to their native land has become not contractual but sacramental. We may say that flags are rags, that frontiers are fictions, but the very men who have said it for half their lives are dying for a rag, and being rent in pieces for a fiction even as I write. When the battle-trumpet blew in 1914 modern humanity had grouped itself into nations almost before it knew what it had done. If the same sound is heard a thousand years hence, there is no sign in the world to suggest to any rational man that humanity will not do exactly the same thing. But even if this great and strange development be not enduring, the point is that it is felt as enduring. It is hard to give a definition of loyalty, but perhaps we come near it if we call it the thing which operates where an obligation is felt to be unlimited. And the minimum of duty or even decency asked of a patriot is the maximum that is asked by the most miraculous view of marriage. The recognized reality of patriotism is not mere citizenship. The recognized reality of patriotism is for better for worse, for richer for poorer, in sickness and in health, in national growth and glory and in national disgrace and decline; it is not to travel in the ship of state as a passenger, but if need be to go down with the ship.

It is needless to tell here again the tale of that earthquake episode in which a clearance in the earth and sky, above the confusion and abasement of the crowns, showed the commanding figure of a woman of the people. She was, in her own living loneliness, a French Revolution. She was the proof that a certain power was not in the French kings or in the French knights, but in the French. But the fact that she saw something above her that was other than the sky, the fact that she lived the life of a saint and died the death of a martyr, probably stamped the new national sentiment with a sacred seal. And the fact that she fought for a defeated country, and, even though it was victorious, was herself ultimately defeated, defines that darker element of devotion of which I spoke above, which makes even pessimism consistent with patriotism. It is more appropriate in this place to consider the ultimate reaction of this sacrifice upon the romance and the realities of England.

I have never counted it a patriotic part to plaster my own country with conventional and unconvincing compliments; but no one can understand England who does not understand that such an episode as this, in which she was so clearly in the wrong, has yet been ultimately linked up with a curious quality in which she is rather unusually in the right. No one candidly comparing us with other countries can say we have specially failed to build the sepulchres of the prophets we stoned, or even the prophets who stoned us. The English historical tradition has at least a loose large-mindedness which always finally falls into the praise not only of great foreigners but great foes. Often along with much injustice it has an illogical generosity; and while it will dismiss a great people with mere ignorance, it treats a great personality with hearty hero-worship. There are more examples than one even in this chapter, for our books may well make out Wallace a better man than he was, as they afterwards assigned to Washington an even better cause than he had. Thackeray smiled at Miss Jane Porter's picture of Wallace, going into war weeping with a cambric pocket-handkerchief; but her attitude was more English and not less accurate. For her idealization was, if anything, nearer the truth than Thackeray's own notion of a mediævalism of hypocritical hogs-in-armour. Edward, who figures as a tyrant, could weep with compassion; and it is probable enough that Wallace wept, with or without a pocket-handkerchief. Moreover, her romance was a reality, the reality of nationalism; and she knew much more about the Scottish patriots ages before her time than Thackeray did about the Irish patriots immediately under his nose. Thackeray was a great man; but in that matter he was a very small man, and indeed an invisible one. The cases of Wallace and Washington and many others are here only mentioned, however, to suggest an eccentric magnanimity which surely balances some of our prejudices. We have done many foolish things, but we have at least done one fine thing; we have whitewashed our worst enemies. If we have done this for a bold Scottish raider and a vigorous Virginian slave-holder, it may at least show that we are not likely to fail in our final appreciation of the one white figure in the motley processions of war. I believe there to be in modern England something like a universal enthusiasm on this subject. We have seen a great English critic write a book about this heroine, in opposition to a great French critic, solely in order to blame him for not having praised her enough. And I do not believe there lives an Englishman now, who if he had the offer of being an Englishman then, would not discard his chance of riding as the crowned conqueror at the head of all the spears of Agincourt, if he could be that English common soldier of whom tradition tells that he broke his spear asunder to bind it into a cross for Joan of Arc.

10. THE WAR OF THE USURPERS

The poet Pope, though a friend of the greatest of Tory Democrats, Bolingbroke, necessarily lived in a world in which even Toryism was Whiggish. And the Whig as a wit never expressed his political point more clearly than in Pope's line which ran: "The right divine of kings to govern wrong." It will be apparent, when I deal with that period, that I do not palliate the real unreason in divine right as Filmer and some of the pedantic cavaliers construed it. They professed the impossible ideal of "non-resistance" to any national and legitimate power; though I cannot see that even that was so servile and superstitious as the more modern ideal of "non-resistance" even to a foreign and lawless power. But the seventeenth century was an age of sects, that is of fads; and the Filmerites made a fad of divine right. Its roots were older, equally religious but much more realistic; and though tangled with many other and even opposite things of the Middle Ages, ramify through all the changes we have now to consider. The connection can hardly be stated better than by taking Pope's easy epigram and pointing out that it is, after all, very weak in philosophy. "The right divine of kings to govern wrong," considered as a sneer, really evades all that we mean by "a right." To have a right to do a thing is not at all the same as to be right in doing it. What Pope says satirically about a divine right is what we all say quite seriously about a human right. If a man has a right to vote, has he not a right to vote wrong? If a man has a right to choose his wife, has he not a right to choose wrong? I have a right to express the opinion which I am now setting down; but I should hesitate to make the controversial claim that this proves the opinion to be right.

Now mediæval monarchy, though only one aspect of mediæval rule, was roughly represented in the idea that the ruler had a right to rule as a voter has a right to vote. He might govern wrong, but unless he governed horribly and extravagantly wrong, he retained his position of right; as a private man retains his right to marriage and locomotion unless he goes horribly and extravagantly off his head. It was not really even so simple as this; for the Middle Ages were not, as it is often the fashion to fancy, under a single and steely discipline. They were very controversial and therefore very complex; and it is easy, by isolating items whether about *jus divinum* or *primus inter pares*, to maintain that the mediævals were almost anything; it has been seriously maintained that they were all Germans. But it is true that the influence of the Church, though by no means of all the great churchmen, encouraged the sense of a sort of sacrament of government, which was meant to make the monarch terrible and therefore often made the man tyrannical. The disadvantage of such despotism is obvious enough. The precise nature of its advantage must be better understood than it is, not for its own sake so much as for the story we have now to tell.

The advantage of "divine right," or irremovable legitimacy, is this; that there is a limit to the ambitions of the rich. "*Roi ne puis*"; the royal power, whether it was or was not the power of heaven, was in one respect like the power of heaven. It was not for sale. Constitutional moralists have often implied that a tyrant and a rabble have the same vices. It has perhaps been less noticed that a tyrant and a rabble most emphatically have the same virtues. And one virtue which they very markedly share is that neither tyrants nor rabbles are snobs; they do not care a button what they do to wealthy people. It is true that tyranny was sometimes treated as coming from the heavens almost in the lesser and more literal sense of coming from the sky; a man no more expected to be the king than to be the west wind or the morning star. But at least no wicked miller can chain the wind to turn only his own mill; no pedantic scholar can trim the morning star to be his own reading-lamp. Yet something very like this is what really happened to England in the later Middle Ages; and the first sign of it, I fancy, was the fall of Richard II.

Shakespeare's historical plays are something truer than historical; they are traditional; the living memory of many things lingered, though the memory of others was lost. He is right in making Richard II. incarnate the claim to divine right; and Bolingbroke the baronial ambition which ultimately broke up the old mediæval order. But divine right had become at once drier and more fantastic by the time of the Tudors. Shakespeare could not recover the fresh and popular part of the thing; for he came at a later stage in a process of stiffening which is the main thing to be studied in later mediævalism. Richard himself was possibly a wayward and exasperating prince; it might well be the weak link that snapped in the strong chain of the Plantagenets. There may have been a real case against the *coup d'état* which he effected in 1397, and his kinsman Henry of Bolingbroke may have had strong sections of disappointed opinion on his side when he effected in 1399 the first true usurpation in English history. But if we wish to understand that larger tradition which even Shakespeare had lost, we must glance back at something which befell Richard even in the first years of his reign. It was certainly the greatest event of his reign; and it was possibly the greatest event of all the reigns which are rapidly considered in this book. The real English people, the men who work with their hands, lifted their hands to strike their masters, probably for the first and certainly for the last time in history.

Pagan slavery had slowly perished, not so much by decaying as by developing into something better. In one sense it did not die, but rather came to life. The slave-owner was like a man who should set up a row of sticks for a fence, and then find they had struck root and were budding into small trees. They would be at once more valuable and less manageable, especially less portable; and such a difference between a stick and a tree was precisely the difference between a slave and a serf—or even the free peasant which the serf seemed rapidly tending to become. It was, in the best sense of a battered phrase, a social evolution, and it had the great evil of one. The evil was that while it was essentially orderly, it was still literally lawless. That is, the emancipation of the commons had already advanced very far, but it had not yet advanced far enough to be embodied in a law. The custom was "unwritten," like the British Constitution, and (like that evolutionary, not to say evasive entity) could always be overridden by the rich, who now drive their great coaches through Acts of Parliament. The new peasant was still legally a slave, and was to learn it by one of those turns of fortune which confound a foolish faith in the common sense of unwritten constitutions. The French Wars gradually grew to be almost as much of a scourge to England as they were to France. England was despoiled by her own victories; luxury and poverty increased at the extremes of society; and, by a process more proper to an ensuing chapter, the balance of the better mediævalism was lost. Finally, a furious plague, called the Black Death, burst like a blast on the land, thinning the population and throwing the work of the world into ruin. There was a shortage of labour; a difficulty of getting luxuries; and the great lords did what one would expect them to do. They became lawyers, and upholders of the letter of the law. They appealed to a rule already nearly obsolete, to drive the serf back to the more direct servitude of the Dark Ages. They announced their decision to the people, and the people rose in arms.

The two dramatic stories which connect Wat Tyler, doubtfully with the beginning, and definitely with the end of the revolt, are far from unimportant, despite the desire of our present prosaic historians to pretend that all dramatic stories are unimportant.

The tale of Tyler's first blow is significant in the sense that it is not only dramatic but domestic. It avenged an insult to the family, and made the legend of the whole riot, whatever its incidental indecencies, a sort of demonstration on behalf of decency. This is important; for the dignity of the poor is almost unmeaning in modern debates; and an inspector need only bring a printed form and a few long words to do the same thing without having his head broken. The occasion of the protest, and the form which the feudal reaction had first taken, was a Poll Tax; but this was but a part of a general process of pressing the population to servile labour, which fully explains the ferocious language held by the government after the rising had failed; the language in which it threatened to make the state of the serf more servile than before. The facts attending the failure in question are less in dispute. The mediæval populace showed considerable military energy and co-operation, stormed its way to London, and was met outside the city by a company containing the King and the Lord Mayor, who were forced to consent to a parley. The treacherous stabbing of Tyler by the Mayor gave the signal for battle and massacre on the spot. The peasants closed in roaring, "They have killed our leader"; when a strange thing happened; something which gives us a fleeting and a final glimpse of the crowned sacramental man of the Middle Ages. For one wild moment divine right was divine.

The King was no more than a boy; his very voice must have rung out to that multitude almost like the voice of a child. But the power of his fathers and the great Christendom from which he came fell in some strange fashion upon him; and riding out alone before the people, he cried out, "I am your leader"; and himself promised to grant them all they asked. That promise was afterwards broken; but those who see in the breach of it the mere fickleness of the young and frivolous king, are not only shallow but utterly ignorant interpreters of the whole trend of that time. The point that must be seized, if subsequent things are to be seen as they are, is that Parliament certainly encouraged, and Parliament almost certainly obliged, the King to repudiate the people. For when, after the rejoicing revolutionists had disarmed and were betrayed, the King urged a humane compromise on the Parliament, the Parliament furiously refused it. Already Parliament is not merely a governing body but a governing class. Parliament was as contemptuous of the peasants in the fourteenth as of the Chartists in the nineteenth century. This council, first summoned by the king like juries and many other things, to get from plain men rather reluctant evidence about taxation, has already become an object of ambition, and is, therefore, an aristocracy. There is already war, in this case literally to the knife, between the Commons with a large C and the commons with a small one. Talking about the knife, it is notable that the murderer of Tyler was not a mere noble but an elective magistrate of the mercantile oligarchy of London; though there is probably no truth in the tale that his blood-stained dagger figures on the arms of the City of London. The mediæval Londoners were quite capable of assassinating a man, but not of sticking so dirty a knife into the neighbourhood of the cross of their Redeemer, in the place which is really occupied by the sword of St. Paul.

It is remarked above that Parliament was now an aristocracy, being an object of ambition. The truth is, perhaps, more subtle than this; but if ever men yearn to serve on juries we may probably guess that juries are no longer popular. Anyhow, this must be kept in mind, as against the opposite idea of the *jus divinum* or fixed authority, if we would appreciate the fall of Richard. If the thing which dethroned him was a rebellion, it was a rebellion of the parliament, of the thing that had just proved much more pitiless than he towards a rebellion of the people. But this is not the main point. The point is that by the removal of Richard, a step above the parliament became possible for the first time. The transition was tremendous; the crown became an object of ambition. That which one could snatch another could snatch from him; that which the House of Lancaster held merely by force the House of York could take from it by force. The spell of an undethronable thing seated out of reach was broken, and for three unhappy generations adventurers strove and stumbled on a stairway slippery with blood, above which was something new in the mediæval imagination; an empty throne.

It is obvious that the insecurity of the Lancastrian usurper, largely because he was a usurper, is the clue to many things, some of which we should now call good, some bad, all of which we should probably call good or bad with the excessive facility with which we dismiss distant things. It led the Lancastrian House to lean on Parliament, which was the mixed matter we have already seen. It may have been in some ways good for the monarchy, to be checked and challenged by an institution which at least kept something of the old freshness and freedom of speech. It was almost certainly bad for the parliament, making it yet more the ally of the mere ambitious noble, of which we shall see much later. It also led the Lancastrian House to lean on patriotism, which was perhaps more popular; to make English the tongue of the court for the first time, and to reopen the French wars with the fine flag-waving of Agincourt. It led it again to lean on the Church, or rather, perhaps, on the higher clergy, and that in the least worthy aspect of clericalism. A certain morbidity which more and more darkened the end of mediævalism showed itself in new and more careful cruelties against the last crop of heresies. A slight knowledge of the philosophy of these heresies will lend little support to the notion that they were in themselves prophetic of the Reformation. It is hard to see how anybody can call Wycliffe a Protestant unless he calls Palagius or Arius a Protestant; and if John Ball was a Reformer, Latimer was not a Reformer. But though the new heresies did not even hint at the beginning of English Protestantism, they did, perhaps, hint at the end of English Catholicism. Cobham did not light a candle to be handed on to Nonconformist chapels; but Arundel did light a torch, and put it to his own church. Such real unpopularity as did in time attach to the old religious system, and which afterwards became a true national tradition against Mary, was doubtless started by the diseased energy of these fifteenth-century bishops. Persecution can be a philosophy, and a defensible philosophy, but with some of these men persecution was rather a perversion. Across the channel, one of them was presiding at the trial of Joan of Arc.

But this perversion, this diseased energy, is the power in all the epoch that follows the fall of Richard II., and especially in those feuds that found so ironic an imagery in English roses—and thorns. The foreshortening of such a backward glance as this book can alone claim to be, forbids any entrance into the military mazes of the wars of York and Lancaster, or any attempt to follow the thrilling recoveries and revenges which filled the lives of Warwick the Kingmaker and the warlike widow of Henry V. The rivals were not, indeed, as is sometimes exaggeratively implied, fighting for nothing, or even (like the lion and the unicorn) merely fighting for the crown. The shadow of a moral difference can still be traced even in that stormy twilight of a heroic time. But when we have said that Lancaster stood, on the whole, for the new notion of a king propped by parliaments and powerful bishops, and York, on the whole, for the remains of the older idea of a king who permits nothing to come between him and his people, we have said everything of permanent political interest that could be traced by counting all the bows of Barnet or all the lances of Tewkesbury. But this truth, that there was something which can only vaguely be called Tory about the Yorkists, has at least one interest, that it lends a justifiable romance to the last and most remarkable figure of the fighting House of York, with whose fall the Wars of the Roses ended.

If we desire at all to catch the strange colours of the sunset of the Middle Ages, to see what had changed yet not wholly killed chivalry, there is no better study than the riddle of Richard III. Of course, scarcely a line of him was like the caricature with which his much meaner successor placarded the world when he was dead. He was not even a hunchback; he had one shoulder slightly higher than the other, probably the effect of his furious swordsmanship on a naturally slender and sensitive frame. Yet his soul, if not his body, haunts us somehow as the crooked shadow of a straight knight of better days. He was not an ogre shedding rivers of blood; some of the men he executed deserved it as much as any men of that wicked time; and even the tale of his murdered nephews is not certain, and is told by those who also tell us he was born with tusks and was originally covered with hair. Yet a crimson cloud cannot be dispelled from his memory, and, so tainted is the very air of that time with carnage, that we cannot say he was incapable even of the things of which he may have been innocent. Whether or no he was a good man, he was apparently a good king and even a popular one; yet we think of him vaguely, and not, I fancy, untruly, as on sufferance. He anticipated the Renascence in an abnormal enthusiasm for art and music, and he seems to have held to the old paths of religion and charity. He did not pluck perpetually at his sword and dagger because his only pleasure was in cutting throats; he probably did it because he was nervous. It was the age of our first portrait-painting, and a fine contemporary portrait of him throws a more plausible light on this particular detail. For it shows him touching, and probably twisting, a ring on his finger, the very act of a high-strung personality who would also fidget with a dagger. And in his face, as there painted, we can study all that has made it worth while to pause so long upon his name; an atmosphere very different from everything before and after. The face has a remarkable intellectual beauty; but there is something else on the face that is hardly in itself either good or evil, and that thing is death; the death of an epoch, the death of a great civilization, the death of something which once sang to the sun in the canticle of St. Francis and sailed to the ends of the earth in the ships of the First Crusade, but which in peace wearied and turned its weapons inwards, wounded its own brethren, broke its own loyalties, gambled for the crown, and grew feverish even about the creed, and has this one grace among its dying virtues, that its valour is the last to die.

But whatever else may have been bad or good about Richard of Gloucester, there was a touch about him which makes him truly the last of the mediæval kings. It is expressed in the one word which he cried aloud as he struck down foe after foe in the last charge at Bosworth—treason. For him, as for the first Norman kings, treason was the same as treachery; and in this case at least it was the same as treachery. When his nobles deserted him before the battle, he did not regard it as a new political combination, but as the sin of false friends and faithless servants. Using his own voice like the trumpet of a herald, he challenged his rival to a fight as personal as that of two paladins of Charlemagne. His rival did not reply, and was not likely to reply. The modern world had begun. The call echoed unanswered down the ages; for since that day no English king has fought after that fashion. Having slain many, he was himself slain and his diminished force destroyed. So ended the war of the usurpers; and the last and most doubtful of all the usurpers, a wanderer from the Welsh marches, a knight from nowhere, found the crown of England under a bush of thorn.

ii. THE REBELLION OF THE RICH

Sir Thomas More, apart from any arguments about the more mystical meshes in which he was ultimately caught and killed, will be hailed by all as a hero of the New Learning; that great dawn of a more rational daylight which for so many made mediævalism seem a mere darkness. Whatever we think of his appreciation of the Reformation, there will be no dispute about his appreciation of the Renascence. He was above all things a Humanist and a very human one. He was even in many ways very modern, which some rather erroneously suppose to be the same as being human; he was also humane, in the sense of humanitarian. He sketched an ideal, or rather perhaps a fanciful social system, with something of the ingenuity of Mr. H. G. Wells, but essentially with much more than the flippancy attributed to Mr. Bernard Shaw. It is not fair to charge the Utopian notions upon his morality; but their subjects and suggestions mark what (for want of a better word) we can only call his modernism. Thus the immortality of animals is the sort of transcendentalism which savours of evolution; and the grosser jest about the preliminaries of marriage might be taken quite seriously by the students of Eugenics. He suggested a sort of pacifism —though the Utopians had a quaint way of achieving it. In short, while he was, with his friend Erasmus, a satirist of mediæval abuses, few would now deny that Protestantism would be too narrow rather than too broad for him. If he was obviously not a Protestant, there are few Protestants who would deny him the name of a Reformer. But he was an innovator in things more alluring to modern minds than theology; he was partly what we should call a Neo-Pagan. His friend Colet summed up that escape from mediævalism which might be called the passage from bad Latin to good Greek. In our loose modern debates they are lumped together; but Greek learning was the growth of this time; there had always been a popular Latin, if a dog-Latin. It would be nearer the truth to call the mediævals bi-lingual than to call their Latin a dead language. Greek never, of course, became so general a possession; but for the man who got it, it is not too much to say that he felt as if he were in the open air for the first time. Much of this Greek spirit was reflected in More; its universality, its urbanity, its balance of buoyant reason and cool curiosity. It is even probable that he shared some of the excesses and errors of taste which inevitably infected the splendid intellectualism of the reaction against the Middle Ages; we can imagine him thinking gargoyles Gothic, in the sense of barbaric, or even failing to be stirred, as Sydney was, by the trumpet of "Chevy Chase." The wealth of the ancient heathen world, in wit, loveliness, and civic heroism, had so recently been revealed to that generation in its dazzling profusion and perfection, that it might seem a trifle if they did here and there an injustice to the relics of the Dark Ages. When, therefore, we look at the world with the eyes of More we are looking from the widest windows of that time; looking over an English landscape seen for the first time very equally, in the level light of the sun at morning. For what he saw was England of the Renascence; England passing from the mediæval to the modern. Thus he looked forth, and saw many things and said many things; they were all worthy and many witty; but he noted one thing which is at once a horrible fancy and a homely and practical fact. He who looked over that landscape said: "Sheep are eating men."

This singular summary of the great epoch of our emancipation and enlightenment is not the fact usually put first in such very curt historical accounts of it. It has nothing to do with the translation of the Bible, or the character of Henry VIII., or the characters of Henry VIII.'s wives, or the triangular debates between Henry and Luther and the Pope. It was not Popish sheep who were eating Protestant men, or *vice versa*; nor did Henry, at any period of his own brief and rather bewildering papacy, have martyrs eaten by lambs as the heathen had them eaten by lions. What was meant, of course, by this picturesque expression, was that an intensive type of agriculture was giving way to a very extensive type of pasture. Great spaces of England which had hitherto been cut up into the commonwealth of a number of farmers were being laid under the sovereignty of a solitary shepherd. The point has been put, by a touch of epigram rather in the manner of More himself, by Mr. J. Stephen, in a striking essay now, I think, only to be found in the back files of *The New Witness*. He enunciated the paradox that the very much admired individual, who made two blades of grass grow instead of one, was a murderer. In the same article, Mr. Stephen traced the true moral origins of this movement, which led to the growing of so much grass and the murder, or at any rate the destruction, of so much humanity. He traced it, and every true record of that transformation traces it, to the growth of a new refinement, in a sense a more rational refinement, in the governing class. The mediæval lord had been, by comparison, a coarse fellow; he had merely lived in the largest kind of farm-house after the fashion of the largest kind of farmer. He drank wine when he could, but he was quite ready to drink ale; and science had not yet smoothed his paths with petrol. At a time later than this, one of the greatest ladies of England writes to her husband that she cannot come to him because her carriage horses are pulling the plough. In the true Middle Ages the greatest men were even more rudely hampered, but in the time of Henry VIII. the transformation was beginning. In the next generation a phrase was common which is one of the keys of the time, and is very much the key to these more ambitious territorial schemes. This or that great lord was said to be "Italianate." It meant subtler shapes of beauty, delicate and ductile glass, gold and silver not treated as barbaric stones but rather as stems and wreaths of molten metal, mirrors, cards and such trinkets bearing a load of beauty; it meant the perfection of trifles. It was not, as in popular Gothic craftsmanship, the almost unconscious touch of art upon all necessary things: rather it was the pouring of the whole soul of passionately conscious art especially into unnecessary things. Luxury was made alive with a soul. We must remember this real thirst for beauty; for it is an explanation—and an excuse.

The old barony had indeed been thinned by the civil wars that closed at Bosworth, and curtailed by the economical and crafty policy of that unkingly king, Henry VII. He was himself a "new man," and we shall see the barons largely give place to a whole nobility of new men. But even the older families already had their faces set in the newer direction. Some of them, the Howards, for instance, may be said to have figured both as old and new families. In any case the spirit of the whole upper class can be described as increasingly new. The English aristocracy, which is the chief creation of the Reformation, is undeniably entitled to a certain praise, which is now almost universally regarded as very high praise. It was always progressive. Aristocrats are accused of being proud of their ancestors; it can truly be said that English aristocrats have rather been proud of their descendants. For their descendants they planned huge foundations and piled mountains of wealth; for their descendants they fought for a higher and higher place in the government of the state; for their descendants, above all, they nourished every new science or scheme of social philosophy. They seized the vast economic chances of pasturage; but they also drained the fens. They swept away the priests, but they condescended to the philosophers. As the new Tudor house passes through its generations a new and more rationalist civilization is being made; scholars are criticizing authentic texts; sceptics are discrediting not only popish saints but pagan philosophers; specialists are analyzing and rationalizing traditions, and sheep are eating men.

We have seen that in the fourteenth century in England there was a real revolution of the poor. It very nearly succeeded; and I need not conceal the conviction that it would have been the best possible thing for all of us if it had entirely succeeded. If Richard

II. had really sprung into the saddle of Wat Tyler, or rather if his parliament had not unhorsed him when he had got there, if he had confirmed the fact of the new peasant freedom by some form of royal authority, as it was already common to confirm the fact of the Trade Unions by the form of a royal charter, our country would probably have had as happy a history as is possible to human nature. The Renascence, when it came, would have come as popular education and not the culture of a club of æsthetics. The New Learning might have been as democratic as the old learning in the old days of mediæval Paris and Oxford. The exquisite artistry of the school of Cellini might have been but the highest grade of the craft of a guild. The Shakespearean drama might have been acted by workmen on wooden stages set up in the street like Punch and Judy, the finer fulfilment of the miracle play as it was acted by a guild. The players need not have been "the king's servants," but their own masters. The great Renascence might have been liberal with its liberal education. If this be a fancy, it is at least one that cannot be disproved; the mediæval revolution was too unsuccessful at the beginning for any one to show that it need have been unsuccessful in the end. The feudal parliament prevailed, and pushed back the peasants at least into their dubious and half-developed status. More than this it would be exaggerative to say, and a mere anticipation of the really decisive events afterwards. When Henry VIII. came to the throne the guilds were perhaps checked but apparently unchanged, and even the peasants had probably regained ground; many were still theoretically serfs, but largely under the easy landlordism of the abbots; the mediæval system still stood. It might, for all we know, have begun to grow again; but all such speculations are swamped in new and very strange things. The failure of the revolution of the poor was ultimately followed by a counter-revolution; a successful revolution of the rich.

The apparent pivot of it was in certain events, political and even personal. They roughly resolve themselves into two: the marriages of Henry VIII. and the affair of the monasteries. The marriages of Henry VIII. have long been a popular and even a stale joke; and there is a truth of tradition in the joke, as there is in almost any joke if it is sufficiently popular, and indeed if it is sufficiently stale. A jocular thing never lives to be stale unless it is also serious. Henry was popular in his first days, and even foreign contemporaries give us quite a glorious picture of a young prince of the Renascence, radiant with all the new accomplishments. In his last days he was something very like a maniac; he no longer inspired love, and even when he inspired fear, it was rather the fear of a mad dog than of a watch-dog. In this change doubtless the inconsistency and even ignominy of his Bluebeard weddings played a great part. And it is but just to him to say that, perhaps with the exception of the first and the last, he was almost as unlucky in his wives as they were in their husband. But it was undoubtedly the affair of the first divorce that broke the back of his honour, and incidentally broke a very large number of other more valuable and universal things. To feel the meaning of his fury we must realize that he did not regard himself as the enemy but rather as the friend of the Pope; there is a shadow of the old story of Becket. He had defended the Pope in diplomacy and the Church

59

in controversy; and when he wearied of his queen and took a passionate fancy to one of her ladies, Anne Boleyn, he vaguely felt that a rather cynical concession, in that age of cynical concessions, might very well be made to him by a friend. But it is part of that high inconsistency which is the fate of the Christian faith in human hands, that no man knows when the higher side of it will really be uppermost, if only for an instant; and that the worst ages of the Church will not do or say something, as if by accident, that is worthy of the best. Anyhow, for whatever reason, Henry sought to lean upon the cushions of Leo and found he had struck his arm upon the rock of Peter. The Pope denied the new marriage; and Henry, in a storm and darkness of anger, dissolved all the old relations with the Papacy. It is probable that he did not clearly know how much he was doing then; and it is very tenable that we do not know it now. He certainly did not think he was Anti-Catholic; and, in one rather ridiculous sense, we can hardly say that he thought he was anti-papal, since he apparently thought he was a pope. From this day really dates something that played a certain part in history, the more modern doctrine of the divine right of kings, widely different from the mediæval one. It is a matter which further embarrasses the open question about the continuity of Catholic things in Anglicanism, for it was a new note and yet one struck by the older party. The supremacy of the King over the English national church was not, unfortunately, merely a fad of the King, but became partly, and for one period, a fad of the church. But apart from all controverted questions, there is at least a human and historic sense in which the continuity of our past is broken perilously at this point. Henry not only cut off England from Europe, but what was even more important, he cuts off England from England.

The great divorce brought down Wolsey, the mighty minister who had held the scales between the Empire and the French Monarchy, and made the modern balance of power in Europe. He is often described under the dictum of *Ego et Rex Meus*; but he marks a stage in the English story rather because he suffered for it than because he said it. *Ego et Rex Meus* might be the motto of any modern Prime Minister; for we have forgotten the very fact that the word minister merely means servant. Wolsey was the last great servant who could be, and was, simply dismissed; the mark of a monarchy still absolute; the English were amazed at it in modern Germany, when Bismarck was turned away like a butler. A more awful act proved the new force was already inhuman; it struck down the noblest of the Humanists. Thomas More, who seemed sometimes like an Epicurean under Augustus, died the death of a saint under Diocletian. He died gloriously jesting; and the death has naturally drawn out for us rather the sacred savours of his soul; his tenderness and his trust in the truth of God. But for Humanism it must have seemed a monstrous sacrifice; it was somehow as if Montaigne were a martyr. And that is indeed the note; something truly to be called unnatural had already entered the naturalism of the Renascence; and the soul of the great Christian rose against it. He pointed to the sun, saying "I shall be above that fellow" with Franciscan familiarity, which can love nature because it will not worship her. So he left to his king the sun, which for so many weary days and years was to go down only on his wrath.

But the more impersonal process which More himself had observed (as noted at the beginning of this chapter) is more clearly defined, and less clouded with controversies, in the second of the two parts of Henry's policy. There is indeed a controversy about the monasteries; but it is one that is clarifying and settling every day. Now it is true that the Church, by the Renascence period, had reached a considerable corruption; but the real proofs of it are utterly different both from the contemporary despotic pretence and from the common Protestant story. It is wildly unfair, for instance, to quote the letters of bishops and such authorities denouncing the sins of monastic life, violent as they often are. They cannot possibly be more violent than the letters of St. Paul to the purest and most primitive churches; the apostle was there writing to those Early Christians whom all churches idealize; and he talks to them as to cut-throats and thieves. The explanation, for those concerned for such subtleties, may possibly be found in the fact that Christianity is not a creed for good men, but for men. Such letters had been written in all centuries; and even in the sixteenth century they do not prove so much that there were bad abbots as that there were good bishops. Moreover, even those who profess that the monks were profligates dare not profess that they were oppressors; there is truth in Cobbett's point that where monks were landlords, they did not become rack-renting landlords, and could not become absentee landlords. Nevertheless, there was a weakness in the good institutions as well as a mere strength in the bad ones; and that weakness partakes of the worst element of the time. In the fall of good things there is almost always a touch of betrayal from within; and the abbots were destroyed more easily because they did not stand together. They did not stand together because the spirit of the age (which is very often the worst enemy of the age) was the increasing division between rich and poor; and it had partly divided even the rich and poor clergy. And the betrayal came, as it nearly always comes, from that servant of Christ who holds the bag.

To take a modern attack on liberty, on a much lower plane, we are familiar with the picture of a politician going to the great brewers, or even the great hotel proprietors, and pointing out the uselessness of a litter of little public-houses. That is what the Tudor politicians did first with the monasteries. They went to the heads of the great houses and proposed the extinction of the small ones. The great monastic lords did not resist, or, at any rate, did not resist enough; and the sack of the religious houses began. But if the lord abbots acted for a moment as lords, that could not excuse them, in the eyes of much greater lords, for having frequently acted as abbots. A momentary rally to the cause of the rich did not wipe out the disgrace of a thousand petty interferences which had told only to the advantage of the poor; and they were soon to learn that it was no epoch for their easy rule and their careless hospitality. The great houses, now isolated, were themselves brought down one by one; and the beggar, whom the monastery had served as a sort of sacred tavern, came to it at evening and found it a ruin. For a new and wide philosophy was in the world, which still rules our society. By this creed most of the mystical virtues of the old monks have simply been turned into great sins; and the greatest of these is charity.

But the populace which had risen under Richard II. was not yet disarmed. It was trained in the rude discipline of bow and bill, and organized into local groups of town and guild and manor. Over half the counties of England the people rose, and fought one final battle for the vision of the Middle Ages. The chief tool of the new tyranny, a dirty fellow named Thomas Cromwell, was specially singled out as the tyrant, and he was indeed rapidly turning all government into a nightmare. The popular movement was put down partly by force; and there is the new note of modern militarism in the fact that it was put down by cynical professional troops, actually brought in from foreign countries, who destroyed English religion for hire. But, like the old popular rising, it was even more put down by fraud. Like the old rising, it was sufficiently triumphant to force the government to a parley; and the government had to resort to the simple expedient of calming the people with promises, and then proceeding to break first the promises and then the people, after the fashion made familiar to us by the modern politicians in their attitude towards the great strikes. The revolt bore the name of the Pilgrimage of Grace, and its programme was practically the restoration of the old religion. In connection with the fancy about the fate of England if Tyler had triumphed, it proves, I think, one thing; that his triumph, while it might or might not have led to something that could be called a reform, would have rendered quite impossible everything that we now know as the Reformation.

The reign of terror established by Thomas Cromwell became an Inquisition of the blackest and most unbearable sort. Historians, who have no shadow of sympathy with the old religion, are agreed that it was uprooted by means more horrible than have ever, perhaps, been employed in England before or since. It was a government by torturers rendered ubiquitous by spies. The spoliation of the monasteries especially was carried out, not only with a violence which recalled barbarism, but with a minuteness for which there is no other word but meanness. It was as if the Dane had returned in the character of a detective. The inconsistency of the King's personal attitude to Catholicism did indeed complicate the conspiracy with new brutalities towards Protestants; but such reaction as there was in this was wholly theological. Cromwell lost that fitful favour and was executed, but the terrorism went on the more terribly for being simplified to the single vision of the wrath of the King. It culminated in a strange act which rounds off symbolically the story told on an earlier page. For the despot revenged himself on a rebel whose defiance seemed to him to ring down three centuries. He laid waste the most popular shrine of the English, the shrine to which Chaucer had once ridden singing, because it was also the shrine where King Henry had knelt to repent. For three centuries the Church and the people had called Becket a saint, when Henry Tudor arose and called him a traitor. This might well be thought the topmost point of autocracy; and yet it was not really so.

For then rose to its supreme height of self-revelation that still stranger something of which we have, perhaps fancifully, found hints before in this history. The strong king was weak. He was immeasurably weaker than the strong kings of the Middle Ages; and whether or no his failure had been foreshadowed, he failed. The breach he had made in the dyke of the ancient doctrines let in a flood that may almost be said to have washed him away. In a sense he disappeared before he died; for the drama that filled his last days is no longer the drama of his own character. We may put the matter most practically by saying that it is unpractical to discuss whether Froude finds any justification for Henry's crimes in the desire to create a strong national monarchy. For whether or no it was desired, it was not created. Least of all our princes did the Tudors leave behind them a secure central government, and the time when monarchy was at its worst comes only one or two generations before the time when it was weakest. But a few years afterwards, as history goes, the relations of the Crown and its new servants were to be reversed on a high stage so as to horrify the world; and the axe which had been sanctified with the blood of More and soiled with the blood of Cromwell was, at the signal of one of that slave's own descendants, to fall and to kill an English king.

The tide which thus burst through the breach and overwhelmed the King as well as the Church was the revolt of the rich, and especially of the new rich. They used the King's name, and could not have prevailed without his power, but the ultimate effect was rather as if they had plundered the King after he had plundered the monasteries. Amazingly little of the wealth, considering the name and theory of the thing, actually remained in royal hands. The chaos was increased, no doubt, by the fact that Edward VI. succeeded to the throne as a mere boy, but the deeper truth can be seen in the difficulty of drawing any real line between the two reigns. By marrying into the Seymour family, and thus providing himself with a son, Henry had also provided the country with the very type of powerful family which was to rule merely by pillage. An enormous and unnatural tragedy, the execution of one of the Seymours by his own brother, was enacted during the impotence of the childish king, and the successful Seymour figured as Lord Protector, though even he would have found it hard to say what he was protecting, since it was not even his own family. Anyhow, it is hardly too much to say that every human thing was left unprotected from the greed of such cannibal protectors. We talk of the dissolution of the monasteries, but what occurred was the dissolution of the whole of the old civilization. Lawyers and lackeys and money-lenders, the meanest of lucky men, looted the art and economics of the Middle Ages like thieves robbing a church. Their names (when they did not change them) became the names of the great dukes and marquises of our own day. But if we look back and forth in our history, perhaps the most fundamental act of destruction occurred when the armed men of the Seymours and their sort passed from the sacking of the Monasteries to the sacking of the Guilds. The mediæval Trade Unions were struck down, their buildings broken into by the soldiery, and their funds seized by the new nobility. And this simple incident takes all its common meaning out of the assertion (in itself plausible enough) that the Guilds, like everything else at that time, were probably not at their best. Proportion is the only practical thing; and it may be true that Cæsar was not feeling well on the morning of the Ides of March. But simply to say that the Guilds declined, is about as true as saying that Cæsar quietly decayed from purely natural causes at the foot of the statue of Pompey.

12. SPAIN AND THE SCHISM OF NATIONS

The revolution that arose out of what is called the Renascence, and ended in some countries in what is called the Reformation, did in the internal politics of England one drastic and definite thing. That thing was destroying the institutions of the poor. It was not the only thing it did, but it was much the most practical. It was the basis of all the problems now connected with Capital and Labour. How much the theological theories of the time had to do with it is a perfectly fair matter for difference of opinion. But neither party, if educated about the facts, will deny that the same time and temper which produced the religious schism also produced this new lawlessness in the rich. The most extreme Protestant will probably be content to say that Protestantism was not the motive, but the mask. The most extreme Catholic will probably be content to admit that Protestantism was not the sin, but rather the punishment. The most sweeping and shameless part of the process was not complete, indeed, until the end of the eighteenth century, when Protestantism was already passing into scepticism. Indeed a very decent case could be made out for the paradox that Puritanism was first and last a veneer on Paganism; that the thing began in the inordinate thirst for new things in the *noblesse* of the Renascence and ended in the Hell-Fire Club. Anyhow, what was first founded at the Reformation was a new and abnormally powerful aristocracy, and what was destroyed, in an ever-increasing degree, was everything that could be held, directly or indirectly, by the people *in spite of* such an aristocracy. This fact has filled all the subsequent history of our country; but the next particular point in that history concerns the position of the Crown. The King, in reality, had already been elbowed aside by the courtiers who had crowded behind him just before the bursting of the door. The King is left behind in the rush for wealth, and already can do nothing alone. And of this fact the next reign, after the chaos of Edward VI.'s, affords a very arresting proof.

Mary Tudor, daughter of the divorced Queen Katherine, has a bad name even in popular history; and popular prejudice is generally more worthy of study than scholarly sophistry. Her enemies were indeed largely wrong about her character, but they were not wrong about her effect. She was, in the limited sense, a good woman, convinced, conscientious, rather morbid. But it is true that she was a bad queen; bad for many things, but especially bad for her own most beloved cause. It is true, when all is said, that she set herself to burn out "No Popery" and managed to burn it in. The concentration of her fanaticism into cruelty, especially its concentration in particular places and in a short time, did remain like something red-hot in the public memory. It was the first of the series of great historical accidents that separated a real, if not universal, public opinion from the old *régime*. It has been summarized in the death by fire of the three famous martyrs at Oxford; for one of them at least, Latimer, was a reformer of the more robust and human type, though another of them, Cranmer, had been so smooth a snob and coward in the councils of Henry VIII. as to make Thomas Cromwell seem by comparison a man. But of what may be called the Latimer tradition, the saner and more genuine Protestantism, I shall speak later. At the time even the Oxford Martyrs probably produced less pity and revulsion than the massacre in the flames of many more obscure enthusiasts, whose very ignorance and poverty made their cause seem more popular than it really was. But this last ugly feature was brought into sharper relief, and produced more conscious or unconscious bitterness, because of that other great fact of which I spoke above, which is the determining test of this time of transition.

What made all the difference was this: that even in this Catholic reign the property of the Catholic Church could not be restored. The very fact that Mary was a fanatic, and yet this act of justice was beyond the wildest dreams of fanaticism—that is the point. The very fact that she was angry enough to commit wrongs for the Church, and yet not bold enough to ask for the rights of the Church—that is the test of the time. She was allowed to deprive small men of their lives, she was not allowed to deprive great men of their property—or rather of other people's property. She could punish heresy, she could not punish sacrilege. She was forced into the false position of killing men who had not gone to church, and sparing men who had gone there to steal the church ornaments. What forced her into it? Not certainly her own religious attitude, which was almost maniacally sincere; not public opinion, which had naturally much more sympathy for the religious humanities which she did not restore than for the religious inhumanities which she did. The force came, of course, from the new nobility and the new wealth they refused to surrender; and the success of this early pressure proves that the nobility was already stronger than the Crown. The sceptre had only been used as a crowbar to break open the door of a treasure-house, and was itself broken, or at least bent, with the blow.

There is a truth also in the popular insistence on the story of Mary having "Calais" written on her heart, when the last relic of the mediæval conquests reverted to France. Mary had the solitary and heroic half-virtue of the Tudors: she was a patriot. But patriots are often pathetically behind the times; for the very fact that they dwell on old enemies often blinds them to new ones. In a later generation Cromwell exhibited the same error reversed, and continued to keep a hostile eye on Spain when he should have kept it on France. In our own time the Jingoes of Fashoda kept it on France when they ought already to have had it on Germany. With no particular antinational intention, Mary nevertheless got herself into an anti-national position towards the most tremendous international problem of her people. It is the second of the coincidences that confirmed the sixteenth-century change, and the name of it was

65

Spain. The daughter of a Spanish queen, she married a Spanish prince, and probably saw no more in such an alliance than her father had done. But by the time she was succeeded by her sister Elizabeth, who was more cut off from the old religion (though very tenuously attached to the new one), and by the time the project of a similar Spanish marriage for Elizabeth herself had fallen through, something had matured which was wider and mightier than the plots of princes. The Englishman, standing on his little island as on a lonely boat, had already felt falling across him the shadow of a tall ship.

Wooden *clichés* about the birth of the British Empire and the spacious days of Queen Elizabeth have not merely obscured but contradicted the crucial truth. From such phrases one would fancy that England, in some imperial fashion, now first realized that she was great. It would be far truer to say that she now first realized that she was small. The great poet of the spacious days does not praise her as spacious, but only as small, like a jewel. The vision of universal expansion was wholly veiled until the eighteenth century; and even when it came it was far less vivid and vital than what came in the sixteenth. What came then was not Imperialism; it was Anti-Imperialism. England achieved, at the beginning of her modern history, that one thing human imagination will always find heroic—the story of a small nationality. The business of the Armada was to her what Bannockburn was to the Scots, or Majuba to the Boers— a victory that astonished even the victors. What was opposed to them was Imperialism in its complete and colossal sense, a thing unthinkable since Rome. It was, in no overstrained sense, civilization itself. It was the greatness of Spain that was the glory of England. It is only when we realize that the English were, by comparison, as dingy, as undeveloped, as petty and provincial as Boers, that we can appreciate the height of their defiance or the splendour of their escape. We can only grasp it by grasping that for a great part of Europe the cause of the Armada had almost the cosmopolitan common sense of a crusade. The Pope had declared Elizabeth illegitimate—logically, it is hard to see what else he could say, having declared her mother's marriage invalid; but the fact was another and perhaps a final stroke sundering England from the elder world. Meanwhile those picturesque English privateers who had plagued the Spanish Empire of the New World were spoken of in the South simply as pirates, and technically the description was true; only technical assaults by the weaker party are in retrospect rightly judged with some generous weakness. Then, as if to stamp the contrast in an imperishable image, Spain, or rather the empire with Spain for its centre, put forth all its strength, and seemed to cover the sea with a navy like the legendary navy of Xerxes. It bore down on the doomed island with the weight and solemnity of a day of judgment; sailors or pirates struck at it with small ships staggering under large cannon, fought it with mere masses of flaming rubbish, and in that last hour of grapple a great storm arose out of the sea and swept round the island, and the gigantic fleet was seen no more. The uncanny completeness and abrupt silence that swallowed this prodigy touched a nerve that has never ceased to vibrate. The hope of England dates from that hopeless hour, for there is no real hope that has not once been a forlorn hope. The breaking of that vast naval net remained like a sign that the small thing which escaped would survive the greatness. And yet there is truly a sense in which we may never be so small or so great again.

For the splendour of the Elizabethan age, which is always spoken of as a sunrise, was in many ways a sunset. Whether we regard it as the end of the Renascence or the end of the old mediæval civilization, no candid critic can deny that its chief glories ended with it. Let the reader ask himself what strikes him specially in the Elizabethan magnificence, and he will generally find it is something of which there were at least traces in mediæval times, and far fewer traces in modern times. The Elizabethan drama is like one of its own tragedies—its tempestuous torch was soon to be trodden out by the Puritans. It is needless to say that the chief tragedy was the cutting short of the comedy; for the comedy that came to England after the Restoration was by comparison both foreign and frigid. At the best it is comedy in the sense of being humorous, but not in the sense of being happy. It may be noted that the givers of good news and good luck in the Shakespearian love-stories nearly all belong to a world which was passing, whether they are friars or fairies. It is the same with the chief Elizabethan ideals, often embodied in the Elizabethan drama. The national devotion to the Virgin Queen must not be wholly discredited by its incongruity with the coarse and crafty character of the historical Elizabeth. Her critics might indeed reasonably say that in replacing the Virgin Mary by the Virgin Queen, the English reformers merely exchanged a true virgin for a false one. But this truth does not dispose of a true, though limited, contemporary cult. Whatever we think of that particular Virgin Queen, the tragic heroines of the time offer us a whole procession of virgin queens. And it is certain that the mediævals would have understood much better than the moderns the martyrdom of *Measure for Measure*. And as with the title of Virgin, so with the title of Queen. The mystical monarchy glorified in *Richard II.* was soon to be dethroned much more ruinously than in *Richard II.* The same Puritans who tore off the pasteboard crowns of the stage players were also to tear off the real crowns of the kings whose parts they played. All mummery was to be forbidden, and all monarchy to be called mummery.

Shakespeare died upon St. George's Day, and much of what St. George had meant died with him. I do not mean that the patriotism of Shakespeare or of England died; that remained and even rose steadily, to be the noblest pride of the coming times. But much more than patriotism had been involved in that image of St. George to whom the Lion Heart had dedicated England long ago in the deserts of Palestine. The conception of a patron saint had carried from the Middle Ages one very unique and as yet unreplaced idea. It was the idea of variation without antagonism. The Seven Champions of Christendom were multiplied by seventy times seven in the patrons of towns, trades and social types; but the very idea that they were all saints excluded the possibility of ultimate rivalry in the fact that they were all patrons. The Guild of the Shoemakers and the Guild of the Skinners, carrying the badges of St. Crispin and St. Bartholomew, might fight each other in the streets; but they did not believe that St.

Crispin and St. Bartholomew were fighting each other in the skies. Similarly the English would cry in battle on St. George and the French on St. Denis; but they did not seriously believe that St. George hated St. Denis or even those who cried upon St. Denis. Joan of Arc, who was on the point of patriotism what many modern people would call very fanatical, was yet upon this point what most modern people would call very enlightened. Now, with the religious schism, it cannot be denied, a deeper and more inhuman division appeared. It was no longer a scrap between the followers of saints who were themselves at peace, but a war between the followers of gods who were themselves at war. That the great Spanish ships were named after St. Francis or St. Philip was already beginning to mean little to the new England; soon it was to mean something almost cosmically conflicting, as if they were named after Baal or Thor. These are indeed mere symbols; but the process of which they are symbols was very practical and must be seriously followed. There entered with the religious wars the idea which modern science applies to racial wars; the idea of *natural* wars, not arising from a special quarrel but from the nature of the people quarrelling. The shadow of racial fatalism first fell across our path, and far away in distance and darkness something moved that men had almost forgotten.

Beyond the frontiers of the fading Empire lay that outer land, as loose and drifting as a sea, which had boiled over in the barbarian wars. Most of it was now formally Christian, but barely civilized; a faint awe of the culture of the south and west lay on its wild forces like a light frost. This semi-civilized world had long been asleep; but it had begun to dream. In the generation before Elizabeth a great man who, with all his violence, was vitally a dreamer, Martin Luther, had cried out in his sleep in a voice like thunder, partly against the place of bad customs, but largely also against the place of good works in the Christian scheme. In the generation after Elizabeth the spread of the new wild doctrines in the old wild lands had sucked Central Europe into a cyclic war of creeds. In this the house which stood for the legend of the Holy Roman Empire, Austria, the Germanic partner of Spain, fought for the old religion against a league of other Germans fighting for the new. The continental conditions were indeed complicated, and grew more and more complicated as the dream of restoring religious unity receded. They were complicated by the firm determination of France to be a nation in the full modern sense; to stand free and foursquare from all combinations; a purpose which led her, while hating her own Protestants at home, to give diplomatic support to many Protestants abroad, simply because it preserved the balance of power against the gigantic confederation of Spaniards and Austrians. It is complicated by the rise of a Calvinistic and commercial power in the Netherlands, logical, defiant, defending its own independence valiantly against Spain. But on the whole we shall be right if we see the first throes of the modern international problems in what is called the Thirty Years' War; whether we call it the revolt of half-heathens against the Holy Roman Empire, or whether we call it the coming of new sciences, new philosophies, and new ethics from the north. Sweden took a hand in the struggle, and sent a military hero to the help of the newer Germany. But the sort of military heroism everywhere exhibited offered a strange combination of more and more complex strategic science with the most naked and cannibal cruelty. Other forces besides Sweden found a career in the carnage. Far away to the north-east, in a sterile land of fens, a small ambitious family of money-lenders who had become squires, vigilant, thrifty, thoroughly selfish, rather thinly adopted the theories of Luther, and began to lend their almost savage hinds as soldiers on the Protestant side. They were well paid for it by step after step of promotion; but at this time their principality was only the old Mark of Brandenburg. Their own name was Hohenzollern.

13. THE AGE OF THE PURITANS

We should be very much bored if we had to read an account of the most exciting argument or string of adventures in which unmeaning words such as "snark" or "boojum" were systematically substituted for the names of the chief characters or objects in dispute; if we were told that a king was given the alternative of becoming a snark or finally surrendering the boojum, or that a mob was roused to fury by the public exhibition of a boojum, which was inevitably regarded as a gross reflection on the snark. Yet something very like this situation is created by most modern attempts to tell the tale of the theological troubles of the sixteenth and seventeenth centuries, while deferring to the fashionable distaste for theology in this generation—or rather in the last generation. Thus the Puritans, as their name implies, were primarily enthusiastic for what they thought was pure religion; frequently they wanted to impose it on others; sometimes they only wanted to be free to practise it themselves; but in no case can justice be done to what was finest in their characters, as well as first in their thoughts, if we never by any chance ask what "it" was that they wanted to impose or to practise. Now, there was a great deal that was very fine about many of the Puritans, which is almost entirely missed by the modern admirers of the Puritans. They are praised for things which they either regarded with indifference or more often detested with frenzy—such as religious liberty. And yet they are quite insufficiently understood, and are even undervalued, in their logical case for the things they really did care about—such as Calvinism. We make the Puritans picturesque in a way they would violently repudiate, in novels and plays they would have publicly burnt. We are interested in everything about them, except the only thing in which they were interested at all.

We have seen that in the first instance the new doctrines in England were simply an excuse for a plutocratic pillage, and that is the only truth to be told about the matter. But it was far otherwise with the individuals a generation or two after, to whom the wreck of the Armada was already a legend of national deliverance from Popery, as miraculous and almost as remote as the deliverances of which they read so realistically in the Hebrew Books now laid open to them. The august accident of that Spanish defeat may perhaps have coincided only too well with their concentration on the non-Christian parts of Scripture. It may have satisfied a certain Old Testament sentiment of the election of the English being announced in the stormy oracles of air and sea, which was easily turned into that heresy of a tribal pride that took even heavier hold upon the Germans. It is by such things that a civilized state may fall from being a Christian nation to being a Chosen People. But even if their nationalism was of a kind that has ultimately proved perilous to the comity of nations, it still was nationalism. From first to last the Puritans were patriots, a point in which they had a marked superiority over the French Huguenots. Politically, they were indeed at first but one wing of the new wealthy class which had despoiled the Church and were proceeding to despoil the Crown. But while they were all merely the creatures of the great spoliation, many of them were the unconscious creatures of it. They were strongly represented in the aristocracy, but a great number were of the middle classes, though almost wholly the middle classes of the towns. By the poor agricultural population, which was still by far the largest part of the population, they were simply derided and detested. It may be noted, for instance, that, while they led the nation in many of its higher departments, they could produce nothing having the atmosphere of what is rather priggishly called folklore. All the popular tradition there is, as in songs, toasts, rhymes, or proverbs, is all Royalist. About the Puritans we can find no great legend. We must put up as best we can with great literature.

All these things, however, are simply things that other people might have noticed about them; they are not the most important things, and certainly not the things they thought about themselves. The soul of the movement was in two conceptions, or rather in two steps, the first being the moral process by which they arrived at their chief conclusion, and the second the chief conclusion they arrived at. We will begin with the first, especially as it was this which determined all that external social attitude which struck the eye of contemporaries. The honest Puritan, growing up in youth in a world swept bare by the great pillage, possessed himself of a first principle which is one of the three or four alternative first principles which are possible to the mind of man. It was the principle that the mind of man can alone directly deal with the mind of God. It may shortly be called the anti-sacramental principle; but it really applies, and he really applied it, to many things besides the sacraments of the Church. It equally applies, and he equally applied it, to art, to letters, to the love of locality, to music, and even to good manners. The phrase about no priest coming between a man and his Creator is but an impoverished fragment of the full philosophic doctrine; the true Puritan was equally clear that no singer or story-teller or fiddler must translate the voice of God to him into the tongues of terrestrial beauty. It is notable that the one Puritan man of genius in modern times, Tolstoy, did accept this full conclusion; denounced all music as a mere drug, and forbade his own admirers to read his own admirable novels. Now, the English Puritans were not only Puritans but Englishmen, and therefore did not always shine in clearness of head; as we shall see, true Puritanism was rather a Scotch than an English thing. But this was the driving power and the direction; and the doctrine is quite tenable if a trifle insane. Intellectual truth was the only tribute fit for the highest truth of the universe; and the next step in such a study is to observe what the Puritan thought was the truth about that truth. His individual reason, cut loose from instinct as well as tradition, taught him a concept of the omnipotence of God which meant simply the impotence of man. In Luther, the earlier and milder form of the Protestant process only went so far as to say that nothing a man did could help him except his confession of Christ; with Calvin it took the last logical step and said that even this could not help him, since Omnipotence must have disposed of all his destiny beforehand; that men must be created to be lost and saved. In the purer types of whom I speak this logic was white-hot, and we must read the formula into all their parliamentary and legal formulæ. When we read, "The Puritan party demanded reforms in the church," we must understand, "The Puritan party demanded fuller and clearer affirmation that men are created to be lost and saved." When we read, "The Army selected persons for their godliness," we must understand, "The Army selected those persons who seemed most convinced that men are created to be lost and saved." It should be added that this terrible trend was not confined even to Protestant countries; some great Romanists doubtfully followed it until stopped by Rome. It was the spirit of the age, and should be a permanent warning against mistaking the spirit of the age for the immortal spirit of man. For there are now few Christians or non-Christians who can look back at the Calvinism which nearly captured Canterbury and even Rome by the genius and heroism of Pascal or Milton, without crying out, like the lady in Mr. Bernard Shaw's play, "How splendid! How glorious!... and oh what an escape!"

The next thing to note is that their conception of church-government was in a true sense self-government; and yet, for a particular reason, turned out to be a rather selfish self-government. It was equal and yet it was exclusive. Internally the synod or conventicle tended to be a small republic, but unfortunately to be a very small republic. In relation to the street outside the conventicle was not a republic but an aristocracy. It was the most awful of all aristocracies, that of the elect; for it was not a right of birth but a right before birth, and alone of all nobilities it was not laid level in the dust. Hence we have, on the one hand, in the simpler Puritans a ring of real republican virtue; a defiance of tyrants, an assertion of human dignity, but above all an appeal to that first of all republican virtues—publicity. One of the Regicides, on trial for his life, struck the note which all the unnaturalness of his school cannot deprive of nobility: "This thing was not done in a corner." But their most drastic idealism did nothing to recover a ray of the light that at once lightened every man that came into the world, the assumption of a brotherhood in all baptized people. They were, indeed, very like that dreadful scaffold at which the Regicide was not afraid to point. They were certainly public, they may have been public-spirited, they were never popular; and it seems never to have crossed their minds that there was any need to be popular. England was never so little of a democracy as during the short time when she was a republic.

The struggle with the Stuarts, which is the next passage in our history, arose from an alliance, which some may think an accidental alliance, between two things. The first was this intellectual fashion of Calvinism which affected the cultured world as did our recent intellectual fashion of Collectivism. The second was the older thing which had made that creed and perhaps that cultured world possible—the aristocratic revolt under the last Tudors. It was, we might say, the story of a father and a son dragging down the same golden image, but the younger really from hatred of idolatry, and the older solely from love of gold. It is at once the tragedy and the paradox of England that it was the eternal passion that passed, and the transient or terrestrial passion that remained. This was true of England; it was far less true of Scotland; and that is the meaning of the Scotch and English war that ended at Worcester. The first change had indeed been much the same materialist matter in both countries—a mere brigandage of barons; and even John Knox, though he has become a national hero, was an extremely anti-national politician. The patriot party in Scotland was that of Cardinal Beaton and Mary Stuart. Nevertheless, the new creed did become popular in the Lowlands in a positive sense, not even yet known in our own land. Hence in Scotland Puritanism was the main thing, and was mixed with Parliamentary and other oligarchies. In England Parliamentary oligarchy was the main thing, and was mixed with Puritanism. When the storm began to rise against Charles I., after the more or less transitional time of his father, the Scotch successor of Elizabeth, the instances commonly cited mark all the difference between democratic religion and aristocratic politics. The Scotch legend is that of Jenny Geddes, the poor woman who threw a stool at the priest. The English legend is that of John Hampden, the great squire who raised a county against the King. The Parliamentary movement in England was, indeed, almost wholly a thing of squires, with their new allies the merchants. They were squires who may well have regarded themselves as the real and natural leaders of the English; but they were leaders who allowed no mutiny among their followers. There was certainly no Village Hampden in Hampden Village.

The Stuarts, it may be suspected, brought from Scotland a more mediæval and therefore more logical view of their own function; for the note of their nation was logic. It is a proverb that James I. was a Scot and a pedant; it is hardly sufficiently noted that Charles I. also was not a little of a pedant, being very much of a Scot. He had also the virtues of a Scot, courage, and a quite natural dignity and an appetite for the things of the mind. Being somewhat Scottish, he was very un-English, and could not manage a compromise: he tried instead to split hairs, and seemed merely to break promises. Yet he might safely have been far more inconsistent if he had been a little hearty and hazy; but he was of the sort that sees everything in black and white; and it is therefore remembered—especially the black. From the first he fenced with his Parliament as with a mere foe; perhaps he almost felt it as a foreigner. The issue is familiar, and we need not be so careful as the gentleman who wished to finish the chapter in order to find out what happened to Charles I. His minister, the great Strafford, was foiled in an attempt to make him strong in the fashion of a French king, and perished on the scaffold, a frustrated Richelieu. The Parliament claiming the power of the purse, Charles appealed to the power of the sword, and at first carried all before him; but success passed to the wealth of the Parliamentary class, the discipline of the new army, and the patience and genius of Cromwell; and Charles died the same death as his great servant.

Historically, the quarrel resolved itself, through ramifications generally followed perhaps in more detail than they deserve, into the great modern query of whether a King can raise taxes without the consent of his Parliament. The test case was that of Hampden, the great Buckinghamshire magnate, who challenged the legality of a tax which Charles imposed, professedly for a national navy. As even innovators always of necessity seek for sanctity in the past, the Puritan squires made a legend of the mediæval Magna Carta; and they were so far in a true tradition that the concession of John had really been, as we have already noted, anti-despotic without being democratic. These two truths cover two parts of the problem of the Stuart fall, which are of very different certainty, and should be considered separately.

For the first point about democracy, no candid person, in face of the facts, can really consider it at all. It is quite possible to hold that the seventeenth-century Parliament was fighting for the truth; it is not possible to hold that it was fighting for the populace. After the autumn of the Middle Ages Parliament was always actively aristocratic and actively anti-popular. The institution which forbade Charles I. to raise Ship Money was the same institution which previously forbade Richard II. to free the serfs. The group which claimed coal and minerals from Charles I. was the same which afterward claimed the common lands from the village communities. It was the same institution which only two generations before had eagerly helped to destroy, not merely things of popular sentiment like the monasteries, but all the things of popular utility like the guilds and parishes, the local governments of towns and trades. The work of the great lords may have had, indeed it certainly had, another more patriotic and creative side; but it was exclusively the work of the great lords that was done by Parliament. The House of Commons has itself been a House of Lords.

But when we turn to the other or anti-despotic aspect of the campaign against the Stuarts, we come to something much more difficult to dismiss and much more easy to justify. While the stupidest things are said against the Stuarts, the real contemporary case for their enemies is little realized; for it is connected with what our insular history most neglects, the condition of the Continent. It should be remembered that though the Stuarts failed in England they fought for things that succeeded in Europe. These were roughly, first, the effects of the Counter-Reformation, which made the sincere Protestant see Stuart Catholicism not at all as the last flicker of an old flame, but as the spread of a conflagration. Charles II., for instance, was a man of strong, sceptical, and almost irritably humorous intellect, and he was quite certainly, and even reluctantly, convinced of Catholicism as a philosophy. The other and more important matter here was the almost awful autocracy that was being built up in France like a Bastille. It was more logical, and in many ways more equal and even equitable than the English oligarchy, but it really became a tyranny in case of rebellion or even resistance. There were none of the rough English safeguards of juries and good customs of the old common law; there was *lettre de cachet* as unanswerable as magic. The English who defied the law were better off than the French; a French satirist would probably have retorted that it was the English who obeyed the law who were worse off than the French. The ordering of men's normal lives was with the squire; but he was, if anything, more limited when he was the magistrate. He was stronger as master of the village, but actually weaker as agent of the King. In defending this state of things, in short, the Whigs were certainly not defending democracy, but they were in a real sense defending liberty. They were even defending some remains of mediæval liberty, though not the best; the jury though not the guild. Even feudalism had involved a localism not without liberal elements, which lingered in the aristocratic system. Those who loved such things might well be alarmed at the Leviathan of the State, which for Hobbes was a single monster and for France a single man.

As to the mere facts, it must be said again that in so far as Puritanism was pure, it was unfortunately passing. And the very type of the transition by which it passed can be found in that extraordinary man who is popularly credited with making it predominate. Oliver Cromwell is in history much less the leader of Puritanism than the tamer of Puritanism. He was undoubtedly possessed, certainly in his youth, possibly all his life, by the rather sombre religious passions of his period; but as he emerges into importance, he stands more and more for the Positivism of the English as compared with the Puritanism of the Scotch. He is one of the Puritan squires; but he is steadily more of the squire and less of the Puritan; and he points to the process by which the squirearchy became at last merely pagan. This is the key to most of what is praised and most of what is blamed in him; the key to the comparative sanity, toleration and modern efficiency of many of his departures; the key to the comparative coarseness, earthiness, cynicism, and lack of sympathy in many others. He was the reverse of an idealist; and he cannot without absurdity be held up as an ideal; but he was, like most of the squires, a type genuinely English; not without public spirit, certainly not without patriotism. His seizure of personal power, which destroyed an impersonal and ideal government, had something English in its very unreason. The act of killing the King, I fancy, was not primarily his, and certainly not characteristically his. It was a concession to the high inhuman ideals of the tiny group of true Puritans, with whom he had to compromise but with whom he afterwards collided. It was logic rather than cruelty in the act that was not Cromwellian; for he treated with bestial cruelty the native Irish, whom the new spiritual exclusiveness regarded as beasts—or as the modern euphemism would put it, as aborigines. But his practical temper was more akin to such human slaughter on what seemed to him the edges of civilization, than to a sort of human sacrifice in the very centre and forum of it; he is not a representative regicide. In a sense that piece of headsmanship was rather above his head. The real regicides did it in a sort of trance or vision; and he was not troubled with visions. But the true collision between the religious and rational sides of the seventeenth-century movement came symbolically on that day of driving storm at Dunbar, when the raving Scotch preachers overruled Leslie and forced him down into the valley to be the victim of the Cromwellian common sense. Cromwell said that God had delivered them into his hand; but it was their own God who delivered them, the dark unnatural God of the Calvinist dreams, as overpowering as a nightmare—and as passing.

It was the Whig rather than the Puritan that triumphed on that day; it was the Englishman with his aristocratic compromise; and even what followed Cromwell's death, the Restoration, was an aristocratic compromise, and even a Whig compromise. The mob might cheer as for a mediæval king; but the Protectorate and the Restoration were more of a piece than the mob understood. Even in the superficial things where there seemed to be a rescue it was ultimately a respite. Thus the Puritan régime had risen chiefly by one thing unknown to mediævalism—militarism. Picked professional troops, harshly drilled but highly paid, were the new and alien instrument by which the Puritans became masters. These were disbanded and their return resisted by Tories and Whigs; but their return seemed always imminent, because it was in the spirit of the new stern world of the Thirty Years' War. A discovery is an incurable disease; and it had been discovered that a crowd could be turned into an iron centipede, crushing larger and looser crowds. Similarly the remains of Christmas were rescued from the Puritans; but they had eventually to be rescued again by Dickens from the Utilitarians, and may yet have to be rescued by somebody from the vegetarians and teetotallers. The strange army passed and vanished almost like a Moslem invasion; but it had made the difference that armed valour and victory always make, if it was but a negative difference. It was the final break in our history; it was a breaker of many things, and perhaps of popular rebellion in our land. It is something of a verbal symbol that these men founded New England in America, for indeed they tried to found it here. By a paradox, there was something prehistoric in the very nakedness of their novelty. Even the old and savage things they invoked became more savage in becoming more new. In observing what is called their Jewish Sabbath, they would have had to stone the strictest Jew. And they (and indeed their age generally) turned witch-burning from an episode to an epidemic. The destroyers and the things destroyed disappeared together; but they remain as something nobler than the nibbling legalism of some of the Whig cynics who continued their work. They were above all things anti-historic, like the Futurists in Italy; and there was this unconscious greatness about them, that their very sacrilege was public and solemn like a sacrament; and they were ritualists even as iconoclasts. It was, properly considered, but a very secondary example of their strange and violent simplicity that one of them, before a mighty mob at Whitehall, cut off the anointed head of the sacramental man of the Middle Ages. For another, far away in the western shires, cut down the thorn of Glastonbury, from which had grown the whole story of Britain.

Whether or no we believe that the Reformation really reformed, there can be little doubt that the Restoration did not really restore. Charles II. was never in the old sense a King; he was a Leader of the Opposition to his own Ministers. Because he was a clever politician he kept his official post, and because his brother and successor was an incredibly stupid politician, he lost it; but the throne was already only one of the official posts. In some ways, indeed, Charles II. was fitted for the more modern world then beginning; he was rather an eighteenth-century than a seventeenth-century man. He was as witty as a character in a comedy; and it was already the comedy of Sheridan and not of Shakespeare. He was more modern yet when he enjoyed the pure experimentalism of the Royal Society, and bent eagerly over the toys that were to grow into the terrible engines of science. He and his brother, however, had two links with what was in England the losing side; and by the strain on these their dynastic cause was lost. The first, which lessened in its practical pressure as time passed, was, of course, the hatred felt for their religion. The second, which grew as it neared the next century, was their tie with the French Monarchy. We will deal with the religious quarrel before passing on to a much more irreligious age; but the truth about it is tangled and far from easy to trace.

The Tudors had begun to persecute the old religion before they had ceased to belong to it. That is one of the transitional complexities that can only be conveyed by such contradictions. A person of the type and time of Elizabeth would feel fundamentally, and even fiercely, that priests should be celibate, while racking and rending anybody caught talking to the only celibate priests. This mystery, which may be very variously explained, covered the Church of England, and in a great degree the people of England. Whether it be called the Catholic continuity of Anglicanism or merely the slow extirpation of Catholicism, there can be no doubt that a parson like Herrick, for instance, as late as the Civil War, was stuffed with "superstitions" which were Catholic in the extreme sense we should now call Continental. Yet many similar parsons had already a parallel and opposite passion, and thought of Continental Catholicism not even as the errant Church of Christ, but as the consistent Church of Antichrist. It is, therefore, very hard now to guess the proportion of Protestantism; but there is no doubt about its presence, especially its presence in centres of importance like London. By the time of Charles II., after the purge of the Puritan Terror, it had become something at least more inherent and human than the mere exclusiveness of Calvinist creeds or the craft of Tudor nobles. The Monmouth rebellion showed that it had a popular, though an insufficiently popular, backing. The "No Popery" force became the crowd if it never became the people. It was, perhaps, increasingly an urban crowd, and was subject to those epidemics of detailed delusion with which sensational journalism plays on the urban crowds of to-day. One of these scares and scoops (not to add the less technical name of lies) was the Popish Plot, a storm weathered warily by Charles II. Another was the Tale of the Warming Pan, or the bogus heir to the throne, a storm that finally swept away James II.

The last blow, however, could hardly have fallen but for one of those illogical but almost lovable localisms to which the English temperament is prone. The debate about the Church of England, then and now, differs from most debates in one vital point. It is not a debate about what an institution ought to do, or whether that institution ought to alter, but about what that institution actually is. One party, then as now, only cared for it because it was Catholic, and the other only cared for it because it was Protestant. Now, something had certainly happened to the English quite inconceivable to the Scotch or the Irish. Masses of common people loved the Church of England without having even decided what it was. It had a hold different indeed from that of the mediæval Church, but also very different from the barren prestige of gentility which clung to it in the succeeding century. Macaulay, with a widely different purpose in mind, devotes some pages to proving that an Anglican clergyman was socially a mere upper servant in the seventeenth century. He is probably right; but he does not guess that this was but the degenerate continuity of the more democratic priesthood of the Middle Ages. A priest was not treated as a gentleman; but a peasant was treated as a priest. And in England then, as in Europe now, many entertained the fancy that priesthood was a higher thing than gentility. In short, the national church was then at least really national, in a fashion that was emotionally vivid though intellectually vague. When, therefore, James II. seemed to menace this practising communion, he aroused something at least more popular than the mere priggishness of the Whig lords. To this must be added a fact generally forgotten. I mean the fact that the influence then called Popish was then in a real sense regarded as revolutionary. The Jesuit seemed to the English not merely a conspirator but a sort of anarchist. There is something appalling about abstract speculations to many Englishmen; and the abstract speculations of Jesuits like Suarez dealt with extreme democracy and things undreamed of here. The last Stuart proposals for toleration seemed thus to many as vast and empty as atheism. The only seventeenth-century Englishmen who had something of this transcendental abstraction were the Quakers; and the cosy English compromise shuddered when the two things shook hands. For it was something much more than a Stuart intrigue which made these philosophical extremes meet, merely because they were philosophical; and which brought the weary but humorous mind of Charles II. into alliance with the subtle and detached spirit of William Penn.

Much of England, then, was really alarmed at the Stuart scheme of toleration, sincere or insincere, because it seemed theoretical and therefore fanciful. It was in advance of its age or (to use a more intelligent language) too thin and ethereal for its atmosphere. And to this affection for the actual in the English moderates must be added (in what proportion we know not) a persecuting hatred of Popery almost maniacal but quite sincere. The State had long, as we have seen, been turned to an engine of torture against priests and the friends of priests. Men talk of the Revocation of the Edict of

Nantes; but the English persecutors never had so tolerant an edict to revoke. But at least by this time the English, like the French, persecutors were oppressing a minority. Unfortunately there was another province of government in which they were still more madly persecuting the majority. For it was here that came to its climax and took on its terrific character that lingering crime that was called the government of Ireland. It would take too long to detail the close network of unnatural laws by which that country was covered till towards the end of the eighteenth century; it is enough to say here that the whole attitude to the Irish was tragically typified, and tied up with our expulsion of the Stuarts, in one of those acts that are remembered for ever. James II., fleeing from the opinion of London, perhaps of England, eventually found refuge in Ireland, which took arms in his favour. The Prince of Orange, whom the aristocracy had summoned to the throne, landed in that country with an English and Dutch army, won the Battle of the Boyne, but saw his army successfully arrested before Limerick by the military genius of Patrick Sarsfield. The check was so complete that peace could only be restored by promising complete religious liberty to the Irish, in return for the surrender of Limerick. The new English Government occupied the town and immediately broke the promise. It is not a matter on which there is much more to be said. It was a tragic necessity that the Irish should remember it; but it was far more tragic that the English forgot it. For he who has forgotten his sin is repeating it incessantly for ever.

But here again the Stuart position was much more vulnerable on the side of secular policy, and especially of foreign policy. The aristocrats to whom power passed finally at the Revolution were already ceasing to have any supernatural faith in Protestantism as against Catholicism; but they had a very natural faith in England as against France; and even, in a certain sense, in English institutions as against French institutions. And just as these men, the most unmediæval of mankind, could yet boast about some mediæval liberties, Magna Carta, the Parliament and the Jury, so they could appeal to a true mediæval legend in the matter of a war with France. A typical eighteenth-century oligarch like Horace Walpole could complain that the cicerone in an old church troubled him with traces of an irrelevant person named St. Somebody, when he was looking for the remains of John of Gaunt. He could say it with all the *naïveté* of scepticism, and never dream how far away from John of Gaunt he was really wandering in saying so. But though their notion of mediæval history was a mere masquerade ball, it was one in which men fighting the French could still, in an ornamental way, put on the armour of the Black Prince or the crown of Henry of Monmouth. In this matter, in short, it is probable enough that the aristocrats were popular as patriots will always be popular. It is true that the last Stuarts were themselves far from unpatriotic; and James II. in particular may well be called the founder of the British Navy. But their sympathies were with France, among other foreign countries; they took refuge in France, the elder before and the younger after his period of rule; and France aided the later Jacobite efforts to restore their line. And for the new England, especially the new English nobility, France was the enemy.

78

The transformation through which the external relations of England passed at the end of the seventeenth century is symbolized by two very separate and definite steps; the first the accession of a Dutch king and the second the accession of a German king. In the first were present all the features that can partially make an unnatural thing natural. In the second we have the condition in which even those effecting it can hardly call it natural, but only call it necessary. William of Orange was like a gun dragged into the breach of a wall; a foreign gun indeed, and one fired in a quarrel more foreign than English, but still a quarrel in which the English, and especially the English aristocrats, could play a great part. George of Hanover was simply something stuffed into a hole in the wall by English aristocrats, who practically admitted that they were simply stopping it with rubbish. In many ways William, cynical as he was, carried on the legend of the greater and grimmer Puritanism. He was in private conviction a Calvinist; and nobody knew or cared what George was except that he was not a Catholic. He was at home the partly republican magistrate of what had once been a purely republican experiment, and among the cleaner if colder ideals of the seventeenth century. George was when he was at home pretty much what the King of the Cannibal Islands was when he was at home—a savage personal ruler scarcely logical enough to be called a despot. William was a man of acute if narrow intelligence; George was a man of no intelligence. Above all, touching the immediate effect produced, William was married to a Stuart, and ascended the throne hand-in-hand with a Stuart; he was a familiar figure, and already a part of our royal family. With George there entered England something that had scarcely been seen there before; something hardly mentioned in mediæval or Renascence writing, except as one mentions a Hottentot—the barbarian from beyond the Rhine.

The reign of Queen Anne, which covers the period between these two foreign kings, is therefore the true time of transition. It is the bridge between the time when the aristocrats were at least weak enough to call in a strong man to help them, and the time when they were strong enough deliberately to call in a weak man who would allow them to help themselves. To symbolize is always to simplify, and to simplify too much; but the whole may be well symbolized as the struggle of two great figures, both gentlemen and men of genius, both courageous and clear about their own aims, and in everything else a violent contrast at every point. One of them was Henry St. John, Lord Bolingbroke; the other was John Churchill, the famous and infamous Duke of Marlborough. The story of Churchill is primarily the story of the Revolution and how it succeeded; the story of Bolingbroke is the story of the Counter-Revolution and how it failed.

Churchill is a type of the extraordinary time in this, that he combines the presence of glory with the absence of honour. When the new aristocracy had become normal to the nation, in the next few generations, it produced personal types not only of aristocracy but of chivalry. The Revolution reduced us to a country wholly governed by gentlemen; the popular universities and schools of the Middle Ages, like their guilds and abbeys, had been seized and turned into what they are—factories of gentlemen, when they are not merely factories of snobs. It is hard now to realize that what we call the Public Schools were once undoubtedly public. By the Revolution they were already becoming as private as they are now. But at least in the eighteenth century there were great gentlemen in the generous, perhaps too generous, sense now given to the title. Types not merely honest, but rash and romantic in their honesty, remain in the record with the names of Nelson or of Fox. We have already seen that the later reformers defaced from fanaticism the churches which the first reformers had defaced simply from avarice. Rather in the same way the eighteenth-century Whigs often praised, in a spirit of pure magnanimity, what the seventeenth-century Whigs had done in a spirit of pure meanness. How mean was that meanness can only be estimated by realizing that a great military hero had not even the ordinary military virtues of loyalty to his flag or obedience to his superior officers, that he picked his way through campaigns that have made him immortal with the watchful spirit of a thieving camp-follower. When William landed at Torbay on the invitation of the other Whig nobles, Churchill, as if to add something ideal to his imitation of Iscariot, went to James with wanton professions of love and loyalty, went forth in arms as if to defend the country from invasion, and then calmly handed the army over to the invader. To the finish of this work of art but few could aspire, but in their degree all the politicians of the Revolution were upon this ethical pattern. While they surrounded the throne of James, there was scarcely one of them who was not in correspondence with William. When they afterwards surrounded the throne of William, there was not one of them who was not still in correspondence with James. It was such men who defeated Irish Jacobitism by the treason of Limerick; it was such men who defeated Scotch Jacobitism by the treason of Glencoe.

Thus the strange yet splendid story of eighteenth-century England is one of greatness founded on smallness, a pyramid standing on a point. Or, to vary the metaphor, the new mercantile oligarchy might be symbolized even in the externals of its great sister, the mercantile oligarchy of Venice. The solidity was all in the superstructure; the fluctuation had been all in the foundations. The great temple of Chatham and Warren Hastings was reared in its origins on things as unstable as water and as fugitive as foam. It is only a fancy, of course, to connect the unstable element with something restless and even shifty in the lords of the sea. But there was certainly in the genesis, if not in the later generations of our mercantile aristocracy, a thing only too mercantile; something which had also been urged against a yet older example of that polity, something called *Punica fides*. The great Royalist Strafford, going disillusioned to death, had said, "Put not your trust in princes." The great Royalist Bolingbroke may well be said to have retorted, "And least of all in merchant princes."

Bolingbroke stands for a whole body of conviction which bulked very big in English history, but which with the recent winding of the course of history has gone out of sight. Yet without grasping it we cannot understand our past, nor, I will add, our future. Curiously enough, the best English books of the eighteenth century are crammed with it, yet modern culture cannot see it when it is there. Dr. Johnson is full of it; it is what he meant when he denounced minority rule in Ireland, as well as when he said that the devil was the first Whig. Goldsmith is full of it; it is the whole point of that fine poem "The Deserted Village," and is set out theoretically with great lucidity and spirit in "The Vicar of Wakefield." Swift is full of it; and found in it an intellectual brotherhood-in-arms with Bolingbroke himself. In the time of Queen Anne it was probably the opinion of the majority of people in England. But it was not only in Ireland that the minority had begun to rule.

This conviction, as brilliantly expounded by Bolingbroke, had many aspects; perhaps the most practical was the point that one of the virtues of a despot is distance. It is "the little tyrant of the fields" that poisons human life. The thesis involved the truism that a good king is not only a good thing, but perhaps the best thing. But it also involved the paradox that even a bad king is a good king, for his oppression weakens the nobility and relieves the pressure on the populace. If he is a tyrant he chiefly tortures the torturers; and though Nero's murder of his own mother was hardly perhaps a gain to his soul, it was no great loss to his empire. Bolingbroke had thus a wholly rationalistic theory of Jacobitism. He was, in other respects, a fine and typical eighteenth-century intellect, a free-thinking Deist, a clear and classic writer of English. But he was also a man of adventurous spirit and splendid political courage, and he made one last throw for the Stuarts. It was defeated by the great Whig nobles who formed the committee of the new régime of the gentry. And considering who it was who defeated it, it is almost unnecessary to say that it was defeated by a trick.

The small German prince ascended the throne, or rather was hoisted into it like a dummy, and the great English Royalist went into exile. Twenty years afterwards he reappears and reasserts his living and logical faith in a popular monarchy. But it is typical of the whole detachment and distinction of his mind that for this abstract ideal he was willing to strengthen the heir of the king whom he had tried to exclude. He was always a Royalist, but never a Jacobite. What he cared for was not a royal family, but a royal office. He celebrated it in his great book "The Patriot King," written in exile; and when he thought that George's great-grandson was enough of a patriot, he only wished that he might be more of a king. He made in his old age yet another attempt, with such unpromising instruments as George III. and Lord Bute; and when these broke in his hand he died with all the dignity of the *sed victa Catoni.* The great commercial aristocracy grew on to its full stature. But if we wish to realize the good and ill of its growth, there is no better summary than this section from the first to the last of the foiled *coups d'état* of Bolingbroke. In the first his policy made peace with France, and broke the connection with Austria. In the second his policy again made peace with France, and broke the connection with Prussia. For in that interval the seed of the money-lending squires of Brandenburg had waxed mighty, and had already become that prodigy which has become so enormous a problem in Europe. By the end of this epoch Chatham, who incarnated and even created, at least in a representative sense, all that we call the British Empire, was at the height of his own and his country's glory. He summarized the new England of the Revolution in everything, especially in everything in which that movement seems to many to be intrinsically contradictory and yet was most corporately consistent. Thus he was a Whig, and even in some ways what we should call a Liberal, like his son after him; but he was also an Imperialist and what we should call a Jingo; and the Whig party was consistently the Jingo party. He was an aristocrat, in the sense that all our public men were then aristocrats; but he was very emphatically what may be called a commercialist—one might almost say Carthaginian. In this connection he has the characteristic which perhaps humanized but was not allowed to hamper the aristo- cratic plan; I mean that he could use the middle classes. It was a young soldier of middle rank, James Wolfe, who fell gloriously driving the French out of Quebec; it was a young clerk of the East India Company, Robert Clive, who threw open to the English the golden gates of India. But it was precisely one of the strong points of this eighteenth-century aristocracy that it wielded without friction the wealthier *bour-geoisie*; it was not there that the social cleavage was to come. He was an eloquent parliamentary orator, and though Parliament was as narrow as a senate, it was one of great senators. The very word recalls the roll of those noble Roman phrases they often used, which we are right in calling classic, but wrong in calling cold. In some ways nothing could be further from all this fine if florid scholarship, all this princely and patrician geniality, all this air of freedom and adventure on the sea, than the little inland state of the stingy drill-sergeants of Potsdam, hammering mere savages into mere soldiers. And yet the great chief of these was in some ways like a shadow of Chatham flung across the world—the sort of shadow that is at once an enlargement and a caricature. The English lords, whose paganism was ennobled by patriotism, saw here something drawn out long and thin out of their own theories. What was paganism in Chatham was atheism in Frederick the Great. And what was in the first patriotism was in the second something with no name but Prussianism. The cannibal theory of a commonwealth, that it can of its nature eat other commonwealths, had entered Christendom. Its autocracy and our own aristocracy drew indirectly nearer together, and seemed for a time to be wedded; but not before the great Bolingbroke had made a dying gesture, as if to forbid the banns.

15. THE WAR WITH THE GREAT REPUBLICS

We cannot understand the eighteenth century so long as we suppose that rhetoric is artificial because it is artistic. We do not fall into this folly about any of the other arts. We talk of a man picking out notes arranged in ivory on a wooden piano "with much feeling," or of his pouring out his soul by scraping on cat-gut after a training as careful as an acrobat's. But we are still haunted with a prejudice that verbal form and verbal effect must somehow be hypocritical when they are the link between things so living as a man and a mob. We doubt the feeling of the old-fashioned orator, because his periods are so rounded and pointed as to convey his feeling. Now before any criti- cism of the eighteenth-century worthies must be put the proviso of their perfect artistic sincerity. Their oratory was unrhymed poetry, and it had the humanity of poetry. It was not even unmetrical poetry; that century is full of great phrases, often spoken on the spur of great moments, which have in them the throb and recurrence of song, as of a man thinking to a tune. Nelson's "In honour I gained them, in honour I will die with them," has more rhythm than much that is called *vers libres*. Patrick Henry's "Give me liberty or give me death" might be a great line in Walt Whitman.

It is one of the many quaint perversities of the English to pretend to be bad speakers; but in fact the most English eighteenth-century epoch blazed with brilliant speakers. There may have been finer writing in France; there was no such fine speaking as in England. The Parliament had faults enough, but it was sincere enough to be rhetorical. The Parliament was corrupt, as it is now; though the examples of corruption were then often really made examples, in the sense of warnings, where they are now examples only in the sense of patterns. The Parliament was indifferent to the constituencies, as it is now; though perhaps the constituencies were less indifferent to the Parliament. The Parliament was snobbish, as it is now, though perhaps more respectful to mere rank and less to mere wealth. But the Parliament was a Parliament; it did fulfil its name and duty by talking, and trying to talk well. It did not merely do things because they do not bear talking about—as it does now. It was then, to the eternal glory of our country, a great "talking-shop," not a mere buying and selling shop for financial tips and official places. And as with any other artist, the care the eighteenth-century man expended on oratory is a proof of his sincerity, not a disproof of it. An enthusiastic eulogium by Burke is as rich and elaborate as a lover's sonnet; but it is because Burke is really enthusiastic, like the lover. An angry sentence by Junius is as carefully compounded as a Renascence poison; but it is because Junius is really angry—like the poisoner. Now, nobody who has realized this psychological truth can doubt for a moment that many of the English aristocrats of the eighteenth century had a real enthusiasm for liberty; their voices lift like trumpets upon the very word. Whatever their immediate forbears may have meant, these men meant what they said when they talked of the high memory of Hampden or the majesty of Magna Carta. Those Patriots whom Walpole called the Boys included many who really were patriots—or better still, who really were boys. If we prefer to put it so, among the Whig aristocrats were many who really were Whigs; Whigs by all the ideal definitions which identified the party with a defence of law against tyrants and courtiers. But if anybody deduces, from the fact that the Whig aristocrats were Whigs, any doubt about whether the Whig aristocrats were aristocrats, there is one practical test and reply. It might be tested in many ways: by the game laws and enclosure laws they passed, or by the strict code of the duel and the definition of honour on which they all insisted. But if it be really questioned whether I am right in calling their whole world an aristocracy, and the very reverse of it a democracy, the true historical test is this: that when republicanism really entered the world, they instantly waged two great wars with it—or (if the view be preferred) it instantly waged two great wars with them. America and France revealed the real nature of the English Parliament. Ice may sparkle, but a real spark will show it is only ice. So when the red fire of the Revolution touched the frosty splendours of the Whigs, there was instantly a hissing and a strife; a strife of the flame to melt the ice, of the water to quench the flame.

It has been noted that one of the virtues of the aristocrats was liberty, especially liberty among themselves. It might even be said that one of the virtues of the aristocrats was cynicism. They were not stuffed with our fashionable fiction, with its stiff and wooden figures of a good man named Washington and a bad man named Boney. They at least were aware that Washington's cause was not so obviously white nor Napoleon's so obviously black as most books in general circulation would indicate. They had a natural admiration for the military genius of Washington and Napoleon; they had the most unmixed contempt for the German Royal Family. But they were, as a class, not only against both Washington and Napoleon, but against them both for the same reason. And it was that they both stood for democracy.

Great injustice is done to the English aristocratic government of the time through a failure to realize this fundamental difference, especially in the case of America. There is a wrong-headed humour about the English which appears especially in this, that while they often (as in the case of Ireland) make themselves out right where they were entirely wrong, they are easily persuaded (as in the case of America) to make themselves out entirely wrong where there is at least a case for their having been more or less right. George III.'s Government laid certain taxes on the colonial community on the eastern seaboard of America. It was certainly not self-evident, in the sense of law and precedent, that the imperial government could not lay taxes on such colonists. Nor were the taxes themselves of that practically oppressive sort which rightly raise everywhere the common casuistry of revolution. The Whig oligarchs had their faults, but utter lack of sympathy with liberty, especially local liberty, and with their adventurous kindred beyond the seas, was by no means one of their faults. Chatham, the great chief of the new and very national *noblesse*, was typical of them in being free from the faintest illiberality and irritation against the colonies as such. He would have made them free and even favoured colonies, if only he could have kept them as colonies. Burke, who was then the eloquent voice of Whiggism, and was destined later to show how wholly it was a voice of aristocracy, went of course even further. Even North compromised; and though George III., being a fool, might himself have refused to compromise, he had already failed to effect the Bolingbroke scheme of the restitution of the royal power. The case for the Americans, the real reason for calling them right in the quarrel, was something much deeper than the quarrel. They were at issue, not with a dead monarchy, but with a living aristocracy; they declared war on something much finer and more formidable than poor old George. Nevertheless, the popular tradition, especially in America, has pictured it primarily as a duel of George III. and George Washington; and, as we have noticed more than once, such pictures though figurative are seldom false. King George's head was not much more useful on the throne than it was on the sign-board of a tavern; nevertheless, the sign-board was really a sign, and a sign of the times. It stood for a tavern that sold not English but German beer. It stood for that side of the Whig policy which Chatham showed when he was tolerant to America alone, but intolerant of America when allied with France. That very wooden sign stood, in short, for the same thing as the juncture with Frederick the Great; it stood for that Anglo-German alliance which, at a very much later time in history, was to turn into the world-old Teutonic Race.

Roughly and frankly speaking, we may say that America forced the quarrel. She wished to be separate, which was to her but another phrase for wishing to be free. She was not thinking of her wrongs as a colony, but already of her rights as a republic. The negative effect of so small a difference could never have changed the world, without the positive effect of a great ideal, one may say of a great new religion. The real case for the colonists is that they felt they could be something, which they also felt, and justly, that England would not help them to be. England would probably have allowed the colonists all sorts of concessions and constitutional privileges; but England could not allow the colonists equality: I do not mean equality with her, but even with each other. Chatham might have compromised with Washington, because Washington was a gentleman; but Chatham could hardly have conceived a country not governed by gentlemen. Burke was apparently ready to grant everything to America; but he would not have been ready to grant what America eventually gained. If he had seen American democracy, he would have been as much appalled by it as he was by French democracy, and would always have been by any democracy. In a word, the Whigs were liberal and even generous aristocrats, but they were aristocrats; that is why their concessions were as vain as their conquests. We talk, with a humiliation too rare with us, about our dubious part in the secession of America. Whether it increase or decrease the humiliation I do not know; but I strongly suspect that we had very little to do with it. I believe we counted for uncommonly little in the case. We did not really drive away the American colonists, nor were they driven. They were led on by a light that went before.

That light came from France, like the armies of Lafayette that came to the help of Washington. France was already in travail with the tremendous spiritual revolution which was soon to reshape the world. Her doctrine, disruptive and creative, was widely misunderstood at the time, and is much misunderstood still, despite the splendid clarity of style in which it was stated by Rousseau in the "Contrat Social," and by Jefferson in The Declaration of Independence. Say the very word "equality" in many modern countries, and four hundred fools will leap to their feet at once to explain that some men can be found, on careful examination, to be taller or handsomer than others. As if Danton had not noticed that he was taller than Robespierre, or as if Washington was not well aware that he was handsomer than Franklin. This is no place to expound a philosophy; it will be enough to say in passing, by way of a parable, that when we say that all pennies are equal, we do not mean that they all look exactly the same. We mean that they are absolutely equal in their one absolute character, in the most important thing about them. It may be put practically by saying that they are coins of a certain value, twelve of which go to a shilling. It may be put symbolically, and even mystically, by saying that they all bear the image of the King. And, though the most mystical, it is also the most practical summary of equality that all men bear the image of the King of Kings. Indeed, it is of course true that this idea had long underlain all Christianity, even in institutions less popular in form than were, for instance, the mob of mediæval republics in Italy. A dogma of equal duties implies that of equal rights. I know of no Christian authority that would not admit that it is as wicked to murder a poor man as a rich man, or as bad to burgle an inelegantly furnished house as a tastefully furnished one. But the world had wandered further and further from these truisms, and nobody in the world was further from them than the group of the great English aristocrats. The idea of the equality of men is in substance simply the idea of the importance of man. But it was precisely the notion of the importance of a mere man which seemed startling and indecent to a society whose whole romance and religion now consisted of the importance of a gentleman. It was as if a man had walked naked into Parliament. There is not space here to develop the moral issue in full, but this will suffice to show that the critics concerned about the difference in human types or talents are considerably wasting their time. If they can understand how two coins can count the same though one is bright and the other brown, they might perhaps understand how two men can vote the same though one is bright and the other dull. If, however, they are still satisfied with their solid objection that some men are dull, I can only gravely agree with them, that some men are very dull.

But a few years after Lafayette had returned from helping to found a republic in America he was flung over his own frontiers for resisting the foundation of a republic in France. So furious was the onward stride of this new spirit that the republican of the new world lived to be the reactionary of the old. For when France passed from theory to practice, the question was put to the world in a way not thinkable in connection with the prefatory experiment of a thin population on a colonial coast. The mightiest of human monarchies, like some monstrous immeasurable idol of iron, was melted down in a furnace barely bigger than itself, and recast in a size equally colossal, but in a shape men could not understand. Many, at least, could not understand it, and least of all the liberal aristocracy of England. There were, of course, practical reasons for a continuous foreign policy against France, whether royal or republican. There was primarily the desire to keep any foreigner from menacing us from the Flemish coast; there was, to a much lesser extent, the colonial rivalry in which so much English glory had been gained by the statesmanship of Chatham and the arms of Wolfe and of Clive. The former reason has returned on us with a singular irony; for in order to keep the French out of Flanders we flung ourselves with increasing enthusiasm into a fraternity with the Germans. We purposely fed and pampered the power which was destined in the future to devour Belgium as France would never have devoured it, and threaten us across the sea with terrors of which no Frenchman would ever dream. But indeed much deeper things unified our attitude towards France before and after the Revolution. It is but one stride from despotism to democracy, in logic as well as in history; and oligarchy is equally remote from both. The Bastille fell, and it seemed to an Englishman merely that a despot had turned into a demos. The young Bonaparte rose, and it seemed to an Englishman merely that a demos had once more turned into a despot. He was not wrong in thinking these allotropic forms of the same alien thing; and that thing was equality. For when millions are equally subject to one law, it makes little difference if they are also subject to one lawgiver; the general social life is a level. The one thing that the English have never understood about Napoleon, in all their myriad studies of his mysterious personality, is how impersonal he was. I had almost said how unimportant he was. He said himself, "I shall go down to history with my code in my hand;" but in practical effects, as distinct from mere name and renown, it would be even truer to say that his code will go down to history with his hand set to it in signature— somewhat illegibly. Thus his testamentary law has broken up big estates and encouraged contented peasants in places where his name is cursed, in places where his name is almost unknown. In his lifetime, of course, it was natural that the annihilating splendour of his military strokes should rivet the eye like flashes of lightning; but his rain fell more silently, and its refreshment remained. It is needless to repeat here that after bursting one world-coalition after another by battles that are the masterpieces of the military art, he was finally worn down by two comparatively popular causes, the resistance of Russia and the resistance of Spain. The former was largely, like so much that is Russian, religious; but in the latter appeared most conspicuously that which concerns us here, the valour, vigilance and high national spirit of England in the eighteenth century. The long Spanish campaign tried and made triumphant the great Irish soldier, afterwards known as Wellington; who has become all the more symbolic since he was finally confronted with Napoleon in the last defeat of the latter at Waterloo. Wellington, though too logical to be at all English, was in many ways typical of the aristocracy; he had irony and independence of mind. But if we wish to realize how rigidly such men remained limited by their class, how little they really knew what was happening in their time, it is enough to note that Wellington seems to have thought he had dismissed Napoleon by saying he was not really a gentleman. If an acute and experienced Chinaman were to say of Chinese Gordon, "He is not actually a Mandarin," we should think that the Chinese system deserved its reputation for being both rigid and remote.

But the very name of Wellington is enough to suggest another, and with it the reminder that this, though true, is inadequate. There was some truth in the idea that the Englishman was never so English as when he was outside England, and never smacked so much of the soil as when he was on the sea. There has run through the national psychology something that has never had a name except the eccentric and indeed extraordinary name of Robinson Crusoe; which is all the more English for being quite undiscoverable in England. It may be doubted if a French or German boy especially wishes that his cornland or vineland were a desert; but many an English boy has wished that his island were a desert island. But we might even say that the Englishman was too insular for an island. He awoke most to life when his island was sundered from the foundations of the world, when it hung like a planet and flew like a bird. And, by a contradiction, the real British army was in the navy; the boldest of the islanders were scattered over the moving archipelago of a great fleet. There still lay on it, like an increasing light, the legend of the Armada; it was a great fleet full of the glory of having once been a small one. Long before Wellington ever saw Waterloo the ships had done their work, and shattered the French navy in the Spanish seas, leaving like a light upon the sea the life and death of Nelson, who died with his stars on his bosom and his heart upon his sleeve. There is no word for the memory of Nelson except to call him mythical. The very hour of his death, the very name of his ship, are touched with that epic completeness which critics call the long arm of coincidence and prophets the hand of God. His very faults and failures were heroic, not in a loose but in a classic sense; in that he fell only like the legendary heroes, weakened by a woman, not foiled by any foe among men. And he remains the incarnation of a spirit in the English that is purely poetic; so poetic that it fancies itself a thousand things, and sometimes even fancies itself prosaic. At a recent date, in an age of reason, in a country already calling itself dull and business-like, with top-hats and factory chimneys already beginning to rise like towers of funereal efficiency, this country clergyman's son moved to the last in a luminous cloud, and acted a fairy tale. He shall remain as a lesson to those who do not understand England, and a mystery to those who think they do. In outward action he led his ships to victory and died upon a foreign sea; but symbolically he established something indescribable and intimate, something that sounds like a native proverb; he was the man who burnt his ships, and who for ever set the Thames on fire.

16. ARISTOCRACY AND THE DISCONTENTS

It is the pathos of many hackneyed things that they are intrinsically delicate and are only mechanically made dull. Any one who has seen the first white light, when it comes in by a window, knows that daylight is not only as beautiful but as mysterious as moonlight. It is the subtlety of the colour of sunshine that seems to be colourless. So patriotism, and especially English patriotism, which is vulgarized with volumes of verbal fog and gas, is still in itself something as tenuous and tender as a climate. The name of Nelson, with which the last chapter ended, might very well summarize the matter; for his name is banged and beaten about like an old tin can, while his soul had something in it of a fine and fragile eighteenth-century vase. And it will be found that the most threadbare things contemporary and connected with him have a real truth to the tone and meaning of his life and time, though for us they have too often degenerated into dead jokes. The expression "hearts of oak," for instance, is no unhappy phrase for the finer side of that England of which he was the best expression. Even as a material metaphor it covers much of what I mean; oak was by no means only made into bludgeons, nor even only into battle-ships; and the English gentry did not think it business-like to pretend to be mere brutes. The mere name of oak calls back like a dream those dark but genial interiors of colleges and country houses, in which great gentlemen, not degenerate, almost made Latin an English language and port an English wine. Some part of that world at least will not perish; for its autumnal glow passed into the brush of the great English portrait-painters, who, more than any other men, were given the power to commemorate the large humanity of their own land; immortalizing a mood as broad and soft as their own brush-work. Come naturally, at the right emotional angle, upon a canvass of Gains-borough, who painted ladies like landscapes, as great and as unconscious with repose, and you will note how subtly the artist gives to a dress flowing in the foreground something of the divine quality of distance. Then you will understand another faded phrase and words spoken far away upon the sea; there will rise up quite fresh before you and be borne upon a bar of music, like words you have never heard before: "For England, home, and beauty."

When I think of these things, I have no temptation to mere grumbling at the great gentry that waged the great war of our fathers. But indeed the difficulty about it was something much deeper than could be dealt with by any grumbling. It was an exclusive class, but not an exclusive life; it was interested in all things, though not for all men. Or rather those things it failed to include, through the limitations of this rationalist interval between mediæval and modern mysticism, were at least not of the sort to shock us with superficial inhumanity. The greatest gap in their souls, for those who think it a gap, was their complete and complacent paganism. All their very decencies assumed that the old faith was dead; those who held it still, like the great Johnson, were considered eccentrics. The French Revolution was a riot that broke up the very formal funeral of Christianity; and was followed by various other complications, including the corpse coming to life. But the scepticism was no mere oligarchic orgy; it was not confined to the Hell-Fire Club; which might in virtue of its vivid name be regarded as relatively orthodox. It is present in the mildest middle-class atmosphere; as in the middle-class masterpiece about "Northanger Abbey," where we actually remember it is an antiquity, without ever remembering it is an abbey. Indeed there is no clearer case of it than what can only be called the atheism of Jane Austen.

Unfortunately it could truly be said of the English gentleman, as of another gallant and gracious individual, that his honour stood rooted in dishonour. He was, indeed, somewhat in the position of such an aristocrat in a romance, whose splendour has the dark spot of a secret and a sort of blackmail. There was, to begin with, an uncomfortable paradox in the tale of his pedigree. Many heroes have claimed to be descended from the gods, from beings greater than themselves; but he himself was far more heroic than his ancestors. His glory did not come from the Crusades but from the Great Pillage. His fathers had not come over with William the Conqueror, but only assisted, in a somewhat shuffling manner, at the coming over of William of Orange.

His own exploits were often really romantic, in the cities of the Indian sultans or the war of the wooden ships; it was the exploits of the far-off founders of his family that were painfully realistic. In this the great gentry were more in the position of Napoleonic marshals than of Norman knights, but their position was worse; for the marshals might be descended from peasants and shopkeepers; but the oligarchs were descended from usurers and thieves. That, for good or evil, was the paradox of England; the typical aristocrat was the typical upstart.

But the secret was worse; not only was such a family founded on stealing, but the family was stealing still. It is a grim truth that all through the eighteenth century, all through the great Whig speeches about liberty, all through the great Tory speeches about patriotism, through the period of Wandewash and Plassy, through the period of Trafalgar and Waterloo, one process was steadily going on in the central senate of the nation. Parliament was passing bill after bill for the enclosure, by the great land-lords, of such of the common lands as had survived out of the great communal system of the Middle Ages. It is much more than a pun, it is the prime political irony of our history, that the Commons were destroying the commons. The very word "common," as we have before noted, lost its great moral meaning, and became a mere topographical term for some remaining scrap of scrub or heath that was not worth stealing. In the eighteenth century these last and lingering commons were connected only with stories about highwaymen, which still linger in our literature. The romance of them was a romance of robbers; but not of the real robbers.

This was the mysterious sin of the English squires, that they remained human, and yet ruined humanity all around them. Their own ideal, nay their own reality of life, was really more generous and genial than the stiff savagery of Puritan captains and Prussian nobles; but the land withered under their smile as under an alien frown. Being still at least English, they were still in their way good-natured; but their posi-tion was false, and a false position forces the good-natured into brutality. The French Revolution was the challenge that really revealed to the Whigs that they must make up their minds to be really democrats or admit that they were really aristocrats. They decided, as in the case of their philosophic exponent Burke, to be really aristocrats; and the result was the White Terror, the period of Anti-Jacobin repression which revealed the real side of their sympathies more than any stricken fields in foreign lands. Cobbett, the last and greatest of the yeomen, of the small farming class which the great estates were devouring daily, was thrown into prison merely for protesting against the flogging of English soldiers by German mercenaries. In that savage dispersal of a peaceful meeting which was called the Massacre of Peterloo, English soldiers were indeed employed, though much more in the spirit of German ones. And it is one of the bitter satires that cling to the very continuity of our history, that such suppression of the old yeoman spirit was the work of soldiers who still bore the title of the Yeomanry.

The name of Cobbett is very important here; indeed it is generally ignored because it is important. Cobbett was the one man who saw the tendency of the time as a whole, and challenged it as a whole; consequently he went without support. It is a mark of our whole modern history that the masses are kept quiet with a fight. They are kept quiet by the fight because it is a sham-fight; thus most of us know by this time that the Party System has been popular only in the same sense that a football match is popular. The division in Cobbett's time was slightly more sincere, but almost as superficial; it was a difference of sentiment about externals which divided the old agricultural gentry of the eighteenth century from the new mercantile gentry of the nineteenth. Through the first half of the nineteenth century there were some real disputes between the squire and the merchant. The merchant became converted to the important economic thesis of Free Trade, and accused the squire of starving the poor by dear bread to keep up his agrarian privilege. Later the squire retorted not ineffectively by accusing the merchant of brutalizing the poor by overworking them in his factories to keep up his commercial success. The passing of the Factory Acts was a confession of the cruelty that underlay the new industrial experiments, just as the Repeal of the Corn Laws was a confession of the comparative weakness and unpopularity of the squires, who had destroyed the last remnants of any peasantry that might have defended the field against the factory. These relatively real disputes would bring us to the middle of the Victorian era. But long before the beginning of the Victorian era, Cobbett had seen and said that the disputes were only relatively real. Or rather he would have said, in his more robust fashion, that they were not real at all. He would have said that the agricultural pot and the industrial kettle were calling each other black, when they had both been blackened in the same kitchen. And he would have been substantially right; for the great industrial disciple of the kettle, James Watt (who learnt from it the lesson of the steam engine), was typical of the age in this, that he found the old Trade Guilds too fallen, unfashionable and out of touch with the times to help his discovery, so that he had recourse to the rich minority which had warred on and weakened those Guilds since the Reformation. There was no prosperous peasant's pot, such as Henry of Navarre invoked, to enter into alliance with the kettle. In other words, there was in the strict sense of the word no commonwealth, because wealth, though more and more wealthy, was less and less common. Whether it be a credit or discredit, industrial science and enterprise were in bulk a new experiment of the old oligarchy; and the old oligarchy had always been ready for new experiments—beginning with the Reformation. And it is characteristic of the clear mind which was hidden from many by the hot temper of Cobbett, that he did see the Reformation as the root of both squirearchy and industrialism, and called on the people to break away from both. The people made more effort to do so than is commonly realized. There are many silences in our somewhat snobbish history; and when the educated class can easily suppress a revolt, they can still more easily suppress the record of it. It was so with some of the chief features of that great mediæval revolution the failure of which, or rather the betrayal of which, was the real turning-point of our history. It was so with the revolts against the religious policy of

Henry VIII.; and it was so with the rick-burning and frame-breaking riots of Cobbett's epoch. The real mob reappeared for a moment in our history, for just long enough to show one of the immortal marks of the real mob—ritualism. There is nothing that strikes the undemocratic doctrinaire so sharply about direct democratic action as the vanity or mummery of the things done seriously in the daylight; they astonish him by being as unpractical as a poem or a prayer. The French Revolutionists stormed an empty prison merely because it was large and solid and difficult to storm, and therefore symbolic of the mighty monarchical machinery of which it had been but the shed. The English rioters laboriously broke in pieces a parish grindstone, merely because it was large and solid and difficult to break, and therefore symbolic of the mighty oligarchical machinery which perpetually ground the faces of the poor. They also put the oppressive agent of some landlord in a cart and escorted him round the county, merely to exhibit his horrible personality to heaven and earth. Afterwards they let him go, which marks perhaps, for good or evil, a certain national modification of the movement. There is something very typical of an English revolution in having the tumbril without the guillotine.

Anyhow, these embers of the revolutionary epoch were trodden out very brutally; the grindstone continued (and continues) to grind in the scriptural fashion above referred to, and, in most political crises since, it is the crowd that has found itself in the cart. But, of course, both the riot and repression in England were but shadows of the awful revolt and vengeance which crowned the parallel process in Ireland. Here the terrorism, which was but a temporary and desperate tool of the aristocrats in England (not being, to do them justice, at all consonant to their temperament, which had neither the cruelty and morbidity nor the logic and fixity of terrorism), became in a more spiritual atmosphere a flaming sword of religious and racial insanity. Pitt, the son of Chatham, was quite unfit to fill his father's place, unfit indeed (I cannot but think) to fill the place commonly given him in history. But if he was wholly worthy of his immortality, his Irish expedients, even if considered as immediately defensible, have not been worthy of *their* immortality. He was sincerely convinced of the national need to raise coalition after coalition against Napoleon, by pouring the commercial wealth then rather peculiar to England upon her poorer Allies, and he did this with indubitable talent and pertinacity. He was at the same time faced with a hostile Irish rebellion and a partly or potentially hostile Irish Parliament. He broke the latter by the most indecent bribery and the former by the most indecent brutality, but he may well have thought himself entitled to the tyrant's plea. But not only were his expedients those of panic, or at any rate of peril, but (what is less clearly realized) it is the only real defence of them that they were those of panic and peril. He was ready to emancipate Catholics as such, for religious bigotry was not the vice of the oligarchy; but he was not ready to emancipate Irishmen as such. He did not really want to enlist Ireland like a recruit, but simply to disarm Ireland like an enemy. Hence his settlement was from the first in a false position for settling anything. The Union may have been a necessity, but the Union was not a Union. It was not intended to be one, and nobody has ever treated it as one. We have not only never succeeded in making Ireland English, as Burgundy has been made French, but we have never tried. Burgundy could boast of Corneille, though Corneille was a Norman, but we should smile if Ireland boasted of Shakespeare. Our vanity has involved us in a mere contradiction; we have tried to combine identification with superiority. It is simply weak-minded to sneer at an Irishman if he figures as an Englishman, and rail at him if he figures as an Irishman. So the Union has never even applied English laws to Ireland, but only coercions and concessions both specially designed for Ireland. From Pitt's time to our own this tottering alternation has continued; from the time when the great O'Connell, with his monster meetings, forced our government to listen to Catholic Emancipation to the time when the great Parnell, with his obstruction, forced it to listen to Home Rule, our staggering equilibrium has been maintained by blows from without. In the later nineteenth century the better sort of special treatment began on the whole to increase. Gladstone, an idealistic though inconsistent Liberal, rather belatedly realized that the freedom he loved in Greece and Italy had its rights nearer home, and may be said to have found a second youth in the gateway of the grave, in the eloquence and emphasis of his conversion. And a statesman wearing the opposite label (for what that is worth) had the spiritual insight to see that Ireland, if resolved to be a nation, was even more resolved to be a peasantry. George Wyndham, generous, imaginative, a man among politicians, insisted that the agrarian agony of evictions, shootings, and rack-rentings should end with the individual Irish getting, as Parnell had put it, a grip on their farms. In more ways than one his work rounds off almost romantically the tragedy of the rebellion against Pitt, for Wyndham himself was of the blood of the leader of the rebels, and he wrought the only reparation yet made for all the blood, shamefully shed, that flowed around the fall of FitzGerald.

The effect on England was less tragic; indeed, in a sense it was comic. Wellington, himself an Irishman though of the narrower party, was preeminently a realist, and, like many Irishmen, was especially a realist about Englishmen. He said the army he commanded was the scum of the earth; and the remark is none the less valuable because that army proved itself useful enough to be called the salt of the earth. But in truth it was in this something of a national symbol and the guardian, as it were, of a national secret. There is a paradox about the English, even as distinct from the Irish or the Scotch, which makes any formal version of their plans and principles inevitably unjust to them. England not only makes her ramparts out of rubbish, but she finds ramparts in what she has herself cast away as rubbish. If it be a tribute to a thing to say that even its failures have been successes, there is truth in that tribute. Some of the best colonies were convict settlements, and might be called abandoned convict settlements. The army was largely an army of gaol-birds, raised by gaol-delivery; but it was a good army of bad men; nay, it was a gay army of unfortunate men. This is the colour and the character that has run through the realities of English history, and it can hardly be put in a book, least of all a historical book. It has its flashes in our fantastic fiction and in the songs of the street, but its true medium is conversation. It has no name but incongruity. An illogical laughter survives everything in the English soul. It survived, perhaps, with only too much patience, the time of terrorism in which the more serious Irish rose in revolt. That time was full of a quite topsy-turvey tyranny, and the English humorist stood on his head to suit it. Indeed, he often receives a quite irrational sentence in a police court by saying he will do it on his head. So, under Pitt's coercionist régime, a man was sent to prison for saying that George IV. was fat; but we feel he must have been partly sustained in prison by the artistic contemplation of how fat he was. That sort of liberty, that sort of humanity, and it is no mean sort, did indeed survive all the drift and downward eddy of an evil economic system, as well as the dragooning of a reactionary epoch and the drearier menace of materialistic social science, as embodied in the new Puritans, who have purified themselves even of religion. Under this long process, the worst that can be said is that the English humorist has been slowly driven downwards in the social scale. Falstaff was a knight, Sam Weller was a gentleman's servant, and some of our recent restrictions seem designed to drive Sam Weller to the status of the Artful Dodger. But well it was for us that some such trampled tradition and dark memory of Merry England survived; well for us, as we shall see, that all our social science failed and all our statesmanship broke down before it. For there was to come the noise of a trumpet and a dreadful day of visitation, in which all the daily workers of a dull civilization were to be called out of their houses and their holes like a resurrection of the dead, and left naked under a strange sun with no religion but a sense of humour. And men might know of what nation Shakespeare was, who broke into puns and practical jokes in the darkest passion of his tragedies, if they had only heard those boys in France and Flanders who called out "Early Doors!" themselves in a theatrical memory, as they went so early in their youth to break down the doors of death.

17. THE RETURN OF THE BARBARIAN

The only way to write a popular history, as we have already remarked, would be to write it backwards. It would be to take common objects of our own street and tell the tale of how each of them came to be in the street at all. And for my immediate purpose it is really convenient to take two objects we have known all our lives, as features of fashion or respectability. One, which has grown rarer recently, is what we call a top-hat; the other, which is still a customary formality, is a pair of trousers. The history of these humorous objects really does give a clue to what has happened in England for the last hundred years. It is not necessary to be an æsthete in order to regard both objects as the reverse of beautiful, as tested by what may be called the rational side of beauty. The lines of human limbs can be beautiful, and so can the lines of loose drapery, but not cylinders too loose to be the first and too tight to be the second. Nor is a subtle sense of harmony needed to see that while there are hundreds of differently proportioned hats, a hat that actually grows larger towards the top is somewhat top-heavy. But what is largely forgotten is this, that these two fantastic objects, which now strike the eye as unconscious freaks, were originally conscious freaks. Our ancestors, to do them justice, did not think them casual or commonplace; they thought them, if not ridiculous, at least rococo. The top-hat was the topmost point of a riot of Regency dandyism, and bucks wore trousers while business men were still wearing knee-breeches. It will not be fanciful to see a certain oriental touch in trousers, which the later Romans also regarded as effeminately oriental; it was an oriental touch found in many florid things of the time—in Byron's poems or Brighton Pavilion. Now, the interesting point is that for a whole serious century these instantaneous fantasies have remained like fossils. In the carnival of the Regency a few fools got into fancy dress, and we have all remained in fancy dress. At least, we have remained in the dress, though we have lost the fancy.

I say this is typical of the most important thing that happened in the Victorian time. For the most important thing was that nothing happened. The very fuss that was made about minor modifications brings into relief the rigidity with which the main lines of social life were left as they were at the French Revolution. We talk of the French Revolution as something that changed the world; but its most important relation to England is that it did not change England. A student of our history is concerned rather with the effect it did not have than the effect it did. If it be a splendid fate to have survived the Flood, the English oligarchy had that added splendour. But even for the countries in which the Revolution was a convulsion, it was the last convulsion—until that which shakes the world to-day. It gave their character to all the commonwealths, which all talked about progress, and were occupied in marking time. Frenchmen, under all superficial reactions, remained republican in spirit, as they had been when they first wore top-hats. Englishmen, under all superficial reforms, remained oligarchical in spirit, as they had been when they first wore trousers. Only one power might be said to be growing, and that in a plodding and prosaic fashion—the power in the North-East whose name was Prussia. And the English were more and more learning that this growth need cause them no alarm, since the North Germans were their cousins in blood and their brothers in spirit.

The first thing to note, then, about the nineteenth century is that Europe remained herself as compared with the Europe of the great war, and that England especially remained herself as compared even with the rest of Europe. Granted this, we may give their proper importance to the cautious internal changes in this country, the small conscious and the large unconscious changes. Most of the conscious ones were much upon the model of an early one, the great Reform Bill of 1832, and can be considered in the light of it. First, from the standpoint of most real reformers, the chief thing about the Reform Bill was that it did not reform. It had a huge tide of popular enthusiasm behind it, which wholly disappeared when the people found themselves in front of it. It enfranchised large masses of the middle classes; it disfranchised very definite bodies of the working classes; and it so struck the balance between the conservative and the dangerous elements in the commonwealth that the governing class was rather stronger than before. The date, however, is important, not at all because it was the beginning of democracy, but because it was the beginning of the best way ever discovered of evading and postponing democracy. Here enters the homœopathic treatment of revolution, since so often successful. Well into the next generation Disraeli, the brilliant Jewish adventurer who was the symbol of the English aristocracy being no longer genuine, extended the franchise to the artisans, partly, indeed, as a party move against his great rival, Gladstone, but more as the method by which the old popular pressure was first tired out and then toned down. The politicians said the working-class was now strong enough to be allowed votes. It would be truer to say it was now weak enough to be allowed votes. So in more recent times Payment of Members, which would once have been regarded (and resisted) as an inrush of popular forces, was passed quietly and without resistance, and regarded merely as an extension of parliamentary privileges. The truth is that the old parliamentary oligarchy abandoned their first line of trenches because they had by that time constructed a second line of defence. It consisted in the concentration of colossal political funds in the private and irresponsible power of the politicians, collected by the sale of peerages and more important things, and expended on the jerrymandering of the enormously expensive elections. In the presence of this inner obstacle a vote became about as valuable as a railway ticket when there is a permanent block on the line. The façade and outward form of this new secret government is the merely mechanical application of what is called the Party System. The Party System does not consist, as some suppose, of two parties, but of one. If there were two real parties, there could be no system.

But if this was the evolution of parliamentary reform, as represented by the first Reform Bill, we can see the other side of it in the social reform attacked immediately after the first Reform Bill. It is a truth that should be a tower and a landmark, that one of the first things done by the Reform Parliament was to establish those harsh and dehumanised workhouses which both honest Radicals and honest Tories branded with the black title of the New Bastille. This bitter name lingers in our literature, and can be found by the curious in the works of Carlyle and Hood, but it is doubtless interesting rather as a note of contemporary indignation than as a correct comparison. It is easy to imagine the logicians and legal orators of the parliamentary school of progress finding many points of differentiation and even of contrast. The Bastille was one central institution; the workhouses have been many, and have everywhere transformed local life with whatever they have to give of social sympathy and inspiration. Men of high rank and great wealth were frequently sent to the Bastille; but no such mistake has ever been made by the more business administration of the workhouse. Over the most capricious operations of the *lettres de cachet* there still hovered some hazy traditional idea that a man is put in prison to punish him for something. It was the discovery of a later social science that men who cannot be punished can still be imprisoned. But the deepest and most decisive difference lies in the better fortune of the New Bastille; for no mob has ever dared to storm it, and it never fell.

The New Poor Law was indeed not wholly new in the sense that it was the culmination and clear enunciation of a principle foreshadowed in the earlier Poor Law of Elizabeth, which was one of the many anti-popular effects of the Great Pillage. When the monasteries were swept away and the mediæval system of hospitality destroyed, tramps and beggars became a problem, the solution of which has always tended towards slavery, even when the question of slavery has been cleared of the irrelevant question of cruelty. It is obvious that a desperate man might find Mr. Bumble and the Board of Guardians less cruel than cold weather and the bare ground—even if he were allowed to sleep on the ground, which (by a veritable nightmare of nonsense and injustice) he is not. He is actually punished for sleeping under a bush on the specific and stated ground that he cannot afford a bed. It is obvious, however, that he may find his best physical good by going into the workhouse, as he often found it in pagan times by selling himself into slavery. The point is that the solution remains servile, even when Mr. Bumble and the Board of Guardians ceased to be in a common sense cruel. The pagan might have the luck to sell himself to a kind master. The principle of the New Poor Law, which has so far proved permanent in our society, is that the man lost all his civic rights and lost them solely through poverty. There is a touch of irony, though hardly of mere hypocrisy, in the fact that the Parliament which effected this reform had just been abolishing black slavery by buying out the slave-owners in the British colonies. The slave-owners were bought out at a price big enough to be called blackmail; but it would be misunderstanding the national mentality to deny the sincerity of the sentiment. Wilberforce represented in this the real wave of Wesleyan religion which had made a humane reaction against Calvinism, and was in no mean sense philanthropic. But there is something romantic in the English mind which can always see what is remote. It is the strongest example of what men lose by being long-sighted. It is fair to say that they gain many things also, the poems that are like adventures and the adventures that are like poems. It is a national savour, and therefore in itself neither good nor evil; and it depends on the application whether we find a scriptural text for it in the wish to take the wings of the morning and abide in the uttermost parts of the sea, or merely in the saying that the eyes of a fool are in the ends of the earth.

Anyhow, the unconscious nineteenth-century movement, so slow that it seems stationary, was altogether in this direction, of which workhouse philanthropy is the type. Nevertheless, it had one national institution to combat and overcome; one institution all the more intensely national because it was not official, and in a sense not even political. The modern Trade Union was the inspiration and creation of the English; it is still largely known throughout Europe by its English name. It was the English expression of the European effort to resist the tendency of Capitalism to reach its natural culmination in slavery. In this it has an almost weird psychological interest, for it is a return to the past by men ignorant of the past, like the subconscious action of some man who has lost his memory. We say that history repeats itself, and it is even more interesting when it unconsciously repeats itself. No man on earth is kept so ignorant of the Middle Ages as the British workman, except perhaps the British business man who employs him. Yet all who know even a little of the Middle Ages can see that the modern Trade Union is a groping for the ancient Guild. It is true that those who look to the Trade Union, and even those clear-sighted enough to call it the Guild, are often without the faintest tinge of mediæval mysticism, or even of mediæval morality. But this fact is itself the most striking and even staggering tribute to mediæval morality. It has all the clinching logic of coincidence. If large numbers of the most hard-headed atheists had evolved, out of their own inner consciousness, the notion that a number of bachelors or spinsters ought to live together in celibate groups for the good of the poor, or the observation of certain hours and offices, it would be a very strong point in favour of the monasteries. It would be all the stronger if the atheists had never heard of monasteries; it would be strongest of all if they hated the very name of monasteries. And it is all the stronger because the man who puts his trust in Trades Unions does not call himself a Catholic or even a Christian, if he does call himself a Guild Socialist.

The Trade Union movement passed through many perils, including a ludicrous attempt of certain lawyers to condemn as a criminal conspiracy that Trade Union solidarity, of which their own profession is the strongest and most startling example in the world. The struggle culminated in gigantic strikes which split the country in every direction in the earlier part of the twentieth century. But another process, with much more power at its back, was also in operation. The principle represented by the New Poor Law proceeded on its course, and in one important respect altered its course, though it can hardly be said to have altered its object. It can most correctly be stated by saying that the employers themselves, who already organized business, began to organize social reform. It was more picturesquely expressed by a cynical aristocrat in Parliament who said, "We are all Socialists now." The Socialists, a body of completely sincere men led by several conspicuously brilliant men, had long hammered into men's heads the hopeless sterility of mere non-interference in exchange. The Socialists proposed that the State should not merely interfere in business but should take over the business, and pay all men as equal wage-earners, or at any rate as wage-earners. The employers were not willing to surrender their own position to the State, and this project has largely faded from politics. But the wiser of them were willing to pay better wages, and they were specially willing to bestow various other benefits so long as they were bestowed after the manner of wages. Thus we had a series of social reforms which, for good or evil, all tended in the same direction; the permission to employees to claim certain advantages as employees, and as something permanently different from employers. Of these the obvious examples were Employers' Liability, Old Age Pensions, and, as marking another and more decisive stride in the process, the Insurance Act.

The latter in particular, and the whole plan of the social reform in general, were modelled upon Germany. Indeed the whole English life of this period was overshadowed by Germany. We had now reached, for good or evil, the final fulfilment of that gathering influence which began to grow on us in the seventeenth century, which was solidified by the military alliances of the eighteenth century, and which in the nineteenth century had been turned into a philosophy—not to say a mythology. German metaphysics had thinned our theology, so that many a man's most solemn conviction about Good Friday was that Friday was named after Freya. German history had simply annexed English history, so that it was almost counted the duty of any patriotic Englishman to be proud of being a German. The genius of Carlyle, the culture preached by Matthew Arnold, would not, persuasive as they were, have alone produced this effect but for an external phenomenon of great force. Our internal policy was transformed by our foreign policy; and foreign policy was dominated by the more and more drastic steps which the Prussian, now clearly the prince of all the German tribes, was taking to extend the German influence in the world. Denmark was robbed of two provinces; France was robbed of two provinces; and though the fall of Paris was felt almost everywhere as the fall of the capital of civilization, a thing like the sacking of Rome by the Goths, many of the most influential people in England still saw nothing in it but the solid success of our kinsmen and old allies of Waterloo. The moral methods which achieved it, the juggling with the Augustenburg claim, the forgery of the Ems telegram, were either successfully concealed or were but cloudily appreciated. The Higher Criticism had entered into our ethics as well as our theology. Our view of Europe was also distorted and made disproportionate by the accident of a natural concern for Constantinople and our route to India, which led Palmerston and later Premiers to support the Turk and see Russia as the only enemy. This somewhat cynical reaction was summed up in the strange figure of Disraeli, who made a pro-Turkish settlement full of his native indifference to the Christian subjects of Turkey, and sealed it at Berlin in the presence of Bismarck. Disraeli was not without insight into the inconsistencies and illusions of the English; he said many sagacious things about them, and one especially when he told the Manchester School that their motto was "Peace and Plenty, amid a starving people, and with the world in arms." But what he said about Peace and Plenty might well be parodied as a comment on what he himself said about Peace with Honour. Returning from that Berlin Conference he should have said, "I bring you Peace with Honour; peace with the seeds of the most horrible war of history; and honour as the dupes and victims of the old bully in Berlin."

But it was, as we have seen, especially in social reform that Germany was believed to be leading the way, and to have found the secret of dealing with the economic evil. In the case of Insurance, which was the test case, she was applauded for obliging all her workmen to set apart a portion of their wages for any time of sickness; and numerous other provisions, both in Germany and England, pursued the same ideal, which was that of protecting the poor against themselves. It everywhere involved an external power having a finger in the family pie; but little attention was paid to any friction thus caused, for all prejudices against the process were supposed to be the growth of ignorance. And that ignorance was already being attacked by what was called education—an enterprise also inspired largely by the example, and partly by the commercial competition of Germany. It was pointed out that in Germany governments and great employers thought it well worth their while to apply the grandest scale of organization and the minutest inquisition of detail to the instruction of the whole German race. The government was the stronger for training its scholars as it trained its soldiers; the big businesses were the stronger for manufacturing mind as they manufactured material. English education was made compulsory; it was made free; many good, earnest, and enthusiastic men laboured to create a ladder of standards and examinations, which would connect the cleverest of the poor with the culture of the English universities and the current teaching in history or philosophy. But it cannot be said that the connection was very complete, or the achievement so thorough as the German achievement. For whatever reason, the poor Englishman remained in many things much as his fathers had been, and seemed to think the Higher Criticism too high for him even to criticize.

And then a day came, and if we were wise, we thanked God that we had failed. Education, if it had ever really been in question, would doubtless have been a noble gift; education in the sense of the central tradition of history, with its freedom, its family honour, its chivalry which is the flower of Christendom. But what would our populace, in our epoch, have actually learned if they had learned all that our schools and universities had to teach? That England was but a little branch on a large Teutonic tree; that an unfathomable spiritual sympathy, all-encircling like the sea, had always made us the natural allies of the great folk by the flowing Rhine; that all light came from Luther and Lutheran Germany, whose science was still purging Christianity of its Greek and Roman accretions; that Germany was a forest fated to grow; that France was a dung-heap fated to decay—a dung-heap with a crowing cock on it. What would the ladder of education have led to, except a platform on which a posturing professor proved that a cousin german was the same as a German cousin? What would the guttersnipe have learnt as a graduate, except to embrace a Saxon because he was the other half of an Anglo-Saxon? The day came, and the ignorant fellow found he had other things to learn. And he was quicker than his educated countrymen, for he had nothing to unlearn.

He in whose honour all had been said and sung stirred, and stepped across the border of Belgium. Then were spread out before men's eyes all the beauties of his culture and all the benefits of his organization; then we beheld under a lifting daybreak what light we had followed and after what image we had laboured to refashion ourselves. Nor in any story of mankind has the irony of God chosen the foolish things so catastrophically to confound the wise. For the common crowd of poor and ignorant Englishmen, because they only knew that they were Englishmen, burst through the filthy cobwebs of four hundred years and stood where their fathers stood when they knew that they were Christian men. The English poor, broken in every revolt, bullied by every fashion, long despoiled of property, and now being despoiled of liberty, entered history with a noise of trumpets, and turned themselves in two years into one of the iron armies of the world. And when the critic of politics and literature, feeling that this war is after all heroic, looks around him to find the hero, he can point to nothing but a mob.

18. CONCLUSION

In so small a book on so large a matter, finished hastily enough amid the necessities of an enormous national crisis, it would be absurd to pretend to have achieved proportion; but I will confess to some attempt to correct a disproportion. We talk of historical perspective, but I rather fancy there is too much perspective in history; for perspective makes a giant a pigmy and a pigmy a giant. The past is a giant foreshortened with his feet towards us; and sometimes the feet are of clay. We see too much merely the sunset of the Middle Ages, even when we admire its colours; and the study of a man like Napoleon is too often that of "The Last Phase." So there is a spirit that thinks it reasonable to deal in detail with Old Sarum, and would think it ridiculous to deal in detail with the Use of Sarum; or which erects in Kensington Gardens a golden monument to Albert larger than anybody has ever erected to Alfred. English history is misread especially, I think, because the crisis is missed. It is usually put about the period of the Stuarts; and many of the memorials of our past seem to suffer from the same visitation as the memorial of Mr. Dick. But though the story of the Stuarts was a tragedy, I think it was also an epilogue.

I make the guess, for it can be no more, that the change really came with the fall of Richard II., following on his failure to use mediæval despotism in the interests of mediæval democracy. England, like the other nations of Christendom, had been created not so much by the death of the ancient civilization as by its escape from death, or by its refusal to die. Mediæval civilization had arisen out of the resistance to the barbarians, to the naked barbarism from the North and the more subtle barbarism from the East. It increased in liberties and local government under kings who controlled the wider things of war and taxation; and in the peasant war of the fourteenth century in England, the king and the populace came for a moment into conscious alliance. They both found that a third thing was already too strong for them. That third thing was the aristocracy; and it captured and called itself the Parliament. The House of Commons, as its name implies, had primarily consisted of plain men summoned by the King like jurymen; but it soon became a very special jury. It became, for good or evil, a great organ of government, surviving the Church, the monarchy and the mob; it did many great and not a few good things. It created what we call the British Empire; it created something which was really far more valuable, a new and natural sort of aristocracy, more humane and even humanitarian than most of the aristocracies of the world. It had sufficient sense of the instincts of the people, at least until lately, to respect the liberty and especially the laughter that had become almost the religion of the race. But in doing all this, it deliberately did two other things, which it thought a natural part of its policy; it took the side of the Protestants, and then (partly as a consequence) it took the side of the Germans. Until very lately most intelligent Englishmen were quite honestly convinced that in both it was taking the side of progress against decay. The question which many of them are now inevitably asking themselves, and would ask whether I asked it or no, is whether it did not rather take the side of barbarism against civilization.

At least, if there be anything valid in my own vision of these things, we have returned to an origin and we are back in the war with the barbarians. It falls as naturally for me that the Englishman and the Frenchman should be on the same side as that Alfred and Abbo should be on the same side, in that black century when the barbarians wasted Wessex and besieged Paris. But there are now, perhaps, less certain tests of the spiritual as distinct from the material victory of civilization. Ideas are more mixed, are complicated by fine shades or covered by fine names. And whether the retreating savage leaves behind him the soul of savagery, like a sickness in the air, I myself should judge primarily by one political and moral test. The soul of savagery is slavery. Under all its mask of machinery and instruction, the German regimentation of the poor was the relapse of barbarians into slavery. I can see no escape from it for ourselves in the ruts of our present reforms, but only by doing what the mediæ-vals did after the other barbarian defeat: beginning, by guilds and small independent groups, gradually to restore the personal property of the poor and the personal freedom of the family. If the English really attempt that, the English have at least shown in the war, to any one who doubted it, that they have not lost the courage and capacity of their fathers, and can carry it through if they will. If they do not do so, if they continue to move only with the dead momentum of the social discipline which we learnt from Germany, there is nothing before us but what Mr. Belloc, the discoverer of this great sociological drift, has called the Servile State. And there are moods in which a man, considering that conclusion of our story, is half inclined to wish that the wave of Teutonic barbarism had washed out us and our armies together; and that the world should never know anything more of the last of the English, except that they died for liberty.

Made in the USA
Monee, IL
22 February 2023

28463084R00059